ESSENTIAL OILS
for a Clean and Healthy Home

200+ Amazing Household Uses for TEA TREE OIL,
PEPPERMINT OIL, LAVENDER OIL, and More

KASEY SCHWARTZ
of AllThingsMamma.com

A **adams**media
Avon, Massachusetts

Published by
Adams Media, a division of F+W Media, Inc.
57 Littlefield Street, Avon, MA 02322. U.S.A.
www.adamsmedia.com

ISBN 10: 1-4405-9372-8
ISBN 13: 978-1-4405-9372-7
eISBN 10: 1-4405-9373-6
eISBN 13: 978-1-4405-9373-4

Printed in the United States of America.

10   9   8   7   6   5   4   3   2   1

Cover design by Stephanie Hannus.
Cover images © F+W Media, Inc.

This book is available at quantity discounts for bulk purchases.
For information, please call 1-800-289-0963.

DEDICATION

To my husband, Brian, and to my children, Ella, Andrew, and Sydney: Thank you for being the inspiration for this book, for helping me want to be a better wife and mom, and for helping me make better decisions for our family and finding the ways to do it! Brian: Thank you for loving me and supporting me in all that I do, from reading my blog in the early days and being the lone commenter on a post to helping me bring this book together through your prayers, support, and encouragement. I could never do it without you. I thank God for each of you and for this opportunity every day! I love you!

ACKNOWLEDGMENTS

Thank you to my husband for his never-ending support and encouragement while writing this book and in my life. Without him, I couldn't do half of what I do. And to my kids, Ella, Andrew, and Sydney, for being so understanding about the craziness that goes along with writing a book. I love you all!

Thank you to the team at Adams Media, including my editor, Katie Corcoran Lytle, and my acquisitions editor, Jacqueline Musser. The support and guidance you have given to me every step of the way has been amazing!

CONTENTS

CHAPTER 4: Kitchen 77

CHAPTER 5: Bathroom 111

CHAPTER 6: Laundry 151

PREFACE

Before I had kids I recycled, used some organic products, and read a ton of books and magazines about how to live a more natural lifestyle, but it wasn't until after I had kids that I got really serious about it. I was no longer in charge of just my own health and well-being; I had a husband and three tiny redheads to keep healthy and make decisions for. They were looking to *me* to know how to live. While I knew I wanted to instill in them a love of God, family, and others, I also wanted them to know how to lead the healthiest lives they could by making better choices for themselves—from the food they eat to the products they use—so I set out to change one thing at a time in our household. I didn't try to do a complete overhaul all at once; that never would have worked, and we all would have been overwhelmed. But making small changes one step at a time add up to big changes over time.

My first step was to buy organic food whenever possible. I then replaced our chemical-filled lotions, soaps, and cleaning products with more natural options. And I eventually traded out those store-bought items for products I made myself using all-natural ingredients and essentials oils! The more I changed, the easier it got. It became a habit to use natural products instead of chemical-filled products. And you know what? My family followed. They began to make healthier choices for themselves—even when we weren't together. Now it's natural for us to clean with lemon essential oil or to spray lemongrass essential oil in the house to freshen the air. It's a part of our life, and I feel great knowing that I'm protecting my family the best that I can in our home by choosing eco-friendly, nontoxic products whenever possible. I can't protect them from everything outside our home, but I sure can do my best inside our home. That's my hope for you: that you'll find small changes you can make in your everyday life that will eventually add up to big changes that make a big difference in your health and well-being.

So pick something to try, whether it's the baking soda–based Lavender Carpet Freshener or the lemony Multisurface Cleaner (see recipes in Chapter 3). Each small change is better for your health, which is something to be proud of. I hope that you find this book useful, gain confidence in your ability to naturally handle anything life throws at you in your home, and find some everyday solutions that you just can't be without!

INTRODUCTION

Eucalyptus oil. Lemon oil. Tea tree oil.

You have probably heard about using lavender essential oil to relax, or maybe you've heard of using peppermint to aid digestion, but did you know that you can actually use essential oils around the house to replace nearly every household product you currently use? It's true! There are literally hundreds of uses for essential oils in your home, and throughout *Essential Oils for a Clean and Healthy Home* you'll find more than 200 of those uses to get you started.

Essential oils have potent cleansing and purifying effects—as well as power-ful scents—that boost the strength of the all-natural cleaning products and house-hold remedies that are safe and effective for your whole family. You can use these essential oils in combination with items you probably already have around your home, like baking soda, vinegar, and Castile soap, to create a natural, chemical-free cleaning experience for every room in your house and for every use imagin-able. Chapter 1 tells you everything you need to know about buying essential oils and using them safely, and what oils you should have on hand, and the following chapters include recipes for making your own natural products at home. You'll find recipes for bathroom items like Eucalyptus Toilet Cleaner, Dry Shampoo, and Linen Closet Spray (see recipes in Chapter 5); kitchen and laundry room cleaners like Peppermint Orange Foaming Hand Soap (see recipe in Chapter 4) and Homemade Liquid Laundry Soap (see recipe in Chapter 6); and cleaners and healthy playtime items for your kids and pets like Calming Bubble Bath, All-Natural Toy Cleanser, and Carpet Pet Stain Remover (see recipes in Chapter 7). There are also ways to use essential oils that you may only use occasionally, like the Citronella Camping Spray (see recipe in Chapter 2) and the Tea Tree Mattress Cleaner (see recipe in Chapter 3). You'll also learn how to use lemon essential oil to make Produce Cleaner (see recipe in Chapter 4), and you'll find recipes to help you clean your stainless steel, brass, and granite in the kitchen and bath. I'll even share ways to use essential oils combined with all-natural ingredients in your kids' areas. From getting rid of sticky messes and crayon marks on the walls to cleansing toys safely, we'll discuss all the little tips and tricks for using essential oils to get your home in tip-top, green condition without breaking the bank.

By switching from store-bought products to essential oils for household uses, you'll save time and money, and cut the toxins found in commercial products out of your life. After all, when you control the ingredients in the products you use, you take charge of your health and well-being. So start reading, and you'll soon be on your way to a healthier and happier home with the help of essential oils!

CHAPTER 1

Using Essential Oils in Your Home

You know that you want to use essential oils to clean your kitchen, bathroom, and more. You realize that you can use these oils to keep pests out of your house and out of your life. And you've heard that you can safely use a variety of these oils to keep your home safe and healthy for your kids and pets. But even though you know all this, you're not quite sure how to put these great ideas and information into practice in your home. Don't worry! Figuring out how to use essential oils—or even learning what essential oils really are—may seem overwhelming, but it doesn't have to be. Throughout this chapter, and throughout the book, you'll learn all you need to know to buy and use essential oils safely and correctly to give you the clean and healthy home you've been looking for. Enjoy!

What Are Essential Oils?

Essential oils are natural aromatic compounds found in the seeds, bark, stems, roots, flowers, and other parts of plants. They are primarily extracted through careful steam distillation, but also through cold pressing. And the purest essential oils are far more powerful than the botanicals from which they were extracted. They are very clean, and are immediately absorbed by the skin. Unlike heavy vegetable oils, pure, unadulterated essential oils are translucent and range in color from crystal clear to deep blue. Essential oils are are great way to cleanse and purify every area of your home naturally, and there's a recipe in the following chapters to address nearly every area of your home!

Why Use Essential Oils in Your Home?

Essential oils have been around for thousands of years and have been used in various ways, from treating health ailments to scenting bath products to making natural cleaning products. They are both powerful and fragrant, and many essential oils have cleansing and purifying properties that are perfect for many everyday home uses. By using essential oils in your home, you can remove toxic chemicals that have an unhealthy effect on your home and your health. Essential oils can do the same things chemical cleaners can do but in an all-natural and healthy way!

These natural cleaning and healing properties are great, especially if you, like so many people these days, are looking for a greener, healthier way of doing things. So many store-bought items, ranging from makeup to cleaning products to insect repellants, are packed full of harmful chemicals, toxins, and who knows what else. And why do you want to spend your hard-earned money on potentially harmful products when you can make products that are as effective as they are safe in the comfort of your own home at a portion of the cost?

Essential oils add power to your everyday products, take the place of chemical-laden items, and have many health benefits. So take charge of your health and well-being and save yourself some money by making the move to control the ingredients in the products you use around your children, your home, and on yourself. You won't regret it!

Top Essential Oils for Cleaning

In this book, you'll find healthy home recipes that include a variety of essential oils, but lavender, lemon, orange, peppermint, and tea tree essential oils are used most often. However, there are other essential oils, such as citronella, eucalyptus, and pine, that aren't used as much but are still quite helpful. Here you'll learn about each of them, their main properties, and ways to use them. As you use these essential oils, keep in mind that, even though they are safe to use, you must use care when handling them. Please be sure to educate yourself on the essential oil you're using and refer to the "Essential Oil Safety Tips" section later in this chapter to learn more.

○ **Carrot Seed:** Carrot seed oil is an essential oil that is known to have naturally occurring SPF. Also, carrot seed has been known for its antiseptic, detoxifying, and antioxidant properties.

○ **Citronella:** Historically used to treat people infected with parasites, citronella essential oil is commonly used to deodorize and purify, as well as to repel insects, which makes it perfect for use in any number of the products found throughout the book. Citronella can also be used in the household for its cleansing and purifying benefits.

○ **Clove:** Clove oil, known for its pain relieving properties, is one the most powerful essential oils.

○ **Eucalyptus:** Eucalyptus essential oil is an all-natural, powerful cleansing oil. Use eucalyptus to cut through dirt and grime, and provide clean surfaces anywhere in your home. You can also use eucalyptus to remove odors from any surface in your home by not covering up odors but removing the source of the odor leaving a clean, pleasant scent.

- **Frankincense:** Frankincense oil is known to cleanse and purify, and is a wonderful addition to bath and body recipes as well as home cleansing recipes. It is also wonderful to use for healthy skin and well-being.

- **Lavender:** Lavender is one of the most versatile essential oils of all, and no home should be without it! Lavender can be used to flavor food and beverages, uplift your mood, and even relieve pain. And, because of its cleansing and purifying properties, which work hard to clean, purify, and protect you and your home from dirt and grime, it is perfect for many household remedies covered in this book.

- **Lemon:** Lemon essential oil is widely known for its potent properties and powerful aromatics. Lemon has cleansing and purifying properties, and also helps promote health and energy. Its invigorating aroma will freshen and energize wherever this essential oil is used, which makes it perfect for so many household remedies. Lemon essential oil is also wonderful at breaking up dirt and grime to get things as clean as possible.

- **Lemongrass:** Lemongrass is a wonderful purification oil that is best known for its ability to remove odors and repel insects.

- **Orange:** Orange essential oil has so many benefits, from leaving you feeling happy and uplifted to flavoring drinks and household products. Orange is widely known for its cleaning power as well as its ability to remove any unwanted odors. It is a must-have in any home! Orange essential oil can cut through grease and grime to get your home sparkling clean while leaving a pleasant scent.

- **Peppermint:** Peppermint essential oil is commonly used for flavoring food and beverages, and as an aid in digestion, but it is also wonderful for purifying, as it will remove dirt, grime, and more. When added to household solutions, its uplifting scent will leave your home smelling fresh and clean.

○ **Pine:** Pine oil is a great essential oil for purifying and cleaning, and it's also great at removing odors. Adding it to home cleaning recipes is a great way to boost cleansing power.

○ **Tea Tree:** Tea tree essential oil, also known as melaleuca, has been long valued for its cleansing and purifying properties, which, when added to household remedies, are very powerful at cleaning every area of your home. It is the perfect addition to all of your household remedies.

As you work your way through the book, you'll see these essential oils used over and over again to help you do everything from purify and clean your home to relax or energize your body. But where can you buy essential oils and what should you look for before you purchase?

Purchasing Essential Oils

Essential oils can be purchased in any large grocery store, health food or specialty store, and online. But be aware that while the oils you find in your local store may be less expensive, they could also be full of alcohol, fillers, and ingredients that aren't 100 percent pure. As we mentioned earlier in this chapter, pure essential oils should never be oily or leave a residue. Instead, they should feel clean to the touch and leave a pleasant, fresh scent. Because essential oils are so rapidly absorbed into the skin, you want to make sure the oils you buy are the safest choice for your family, so it's important to do your own research and decide which brand of oil is right for you. Before buying essential oils from a company, ask the following questions:

○ How are plants and herbs grown? Is the land they are grown on free of chemicals and pesticides?

○ Does the company analyze the oil's composition in a lab to test for purity?

- Does the company own its own farms and source the oils from where they originate, or does the company ever purchase oils from outside suppliers? If so, are the farms monitored and tested to make sure that no chemicals or pesticides are added?

- Does the company continuously monitor the process of distillation to make sure that the oils produced from the distillation contain all of the correct therapeutic components?

- Does the company's oil suppliers use extra solvents during the distillation process to extract extra oil from the plants?

- Can the company guarantee that nothing is added to the oils during bottling?

Again, from safety tips to suggestions on a variety of oils you may find helpful, it's beneficial to research any company you are considering. I also cover essential oils on my blog, *All Things Mamma* (*http://allthingsmamma.com*), so be sure to check for further information and uses there as well.

Remember, it's up to you to decide which oil brand is right for you, since not all oils are created equal. Maybe you won't want to use one company exclusively and will instead use several companies that make products you love. Take the time to do your own research and decide which is the right choice for your family.

Essential Oil Safety Tips

Even though essential oils are all-natural, they are quite powerful! It can take up to seventy-five lemons to produce a 15-milliliter bottle of pure lemon essential oil and 27 square feet of lavender plants to produce one 15-milliliter bottle of lavender essential oil, which should give you an idea of just how concentrated essential oils can be. Because of this, you need to use only a small amount for whatever you're making, and you should always handle essential oils with care.

Some essential oils, like cinnamon and oregano, can feel "hot" to the touch and may cause a burning sensation if you touch them with your bare hands or get them in your eyes or other sensitive areas. And, if you get an oil on your skin and you experience a rare reaction such as a rash or burning sensation, discontinue use and consult a professional if it continues. Fortunately, carrier oils such as coconut, almond, olive oil, or grapeseed oil can be used to help dilute the oil on your skin should it feel uncomfortable, so make sure to always have these oils on hand. Here's a quick safety tip guide to consult while using essential oils:

O If you get essential oils in your eyes or other mucous membranes, flush with a vegetable oil, *never* water. Water drives the oil in deeper and will make you more uncomfortable.

O *Always* buy essential oils from a reputable company that sells pure essential oils. Avoid discount or "cheap" essentials oils, as they can contain fillers and chemicals.

O Always dilute essential oils with a carrier oil before putting them on your skin. A good guideline to follow is 1 drop of essential oil to 3–4 drops of a carrier oil, such as coconut, fractionated coconut, almond, grapeseed, or olive oil.

O When adding essential oils to a spray bottle, glass is best as essential oils can break down plastic over time.

O If using an essential oil for cleaning, be sure to try out the recipe on a small spot first before applying it to an entire surface. The recipes found throughout the book shouldn't stain, but it's always best to test the results before large-scale use.

Remember that essential oils are safe to use, but they must be used with caution and care. If you're not sure if an essential oil is right for the use you have in mind, do a little research or consult a professional.

> **TIP** The recipes and formulations found throughout the book are organic in nature and nontoxic, but as with any cleaner in your home, keep them out of reach of children and pets if close contact is not expected. Please use care in mixing and following the intended uses and directions.

Getting Started

Now that you know what essential oils are, where to find them, and what types are the best to use, it's time to get started. Whether you need a home solution for removing stinky odors from shoes or carpets, a detergent for getting your clothes clean the natural way, or even a fun craft project for your kids that is free of chemicals and toxins, you'll find it here!

CHAPTER 2

Pests, Smells, and Other Nuisances

Like it or not, pests, smells, and other unpleasant nuisances exist in and around your home. Take control and remove them from your life with these all-natural, nontoxic remedies using essential oils. From spiders and mice to dust mites and mosquitoes, there's an essential oil to take care of the problem. Stale odors in your home? Simply need to freshen up your closets and drawers? Try an essential oil remedy. Known to remove odors, repel pests, and purify the home, peppermint, orange, lemon, lavender, and citronella can be used in so many ways. Grab your essential oils, buckets and spray bottles, vinegar, and baking soda and get to work the all-natural way. Before long you'll have a clean and green home that's free of pests and smells!

TICK BE GONE

Summer is a wonderful time to be outdoors. But if you're heading out into wooded areas, make sure to take this natural Tick Be Gone with lavender, lemongrass, and citronella essential oils to keep you tick-free.

YIELD: 1¼ cups

¼ cup witch hazel

1 cup distilled water

10 drops lavender essential oil

10 drops lemongrass essential oil

10 drops citronella essential oil

TO MAKE: Combine all ingredients in a spray bottle. Shake well.

TO USE: Spray over hair, clothes, pant cuffs, and shoes. Repeat every couple of hours.

TO STORE: Store indefinitely in spray bottle.

TIP It is best to use distilled water in any recipes you'll be storing because this pure water has gone through a rigorous filtration process to strip it of not only contaminants but also any natural minerals. However, if you're preparing a recipe for a one-time use, regular tap water is fine.

HEALTHY SCALP SHAMPOO

To keep lice at bay, use this homemade shampoo made from tea tree essential oil that is free of chemicals and safe for the whole family.

YIELD: 1 application of Healthy Scalp Shampoo

1–2 drops tea tree essential oil

TO MAKE: Squeeze your normal amount of shampoo into your hand. Then add tea tree essential oil and use your hands to mix into a lather before applying to the scalp

TO USE: Shampoo hair as normal. Rinse well. Style as usual.

VARIATION

If you'd prefer, you can add 10–20 drops of tea tree essential oil to an 8-ounce bottle of shampoo. Mix well by shaking and use as normal instead of adding the essential oil daily.

LICE BE GONE

If you or your kids happen to get lice, don't fret! This all-natural home remedy with tea tree essential oil suffocates and kills lice, making them easier to remove.

YIELD: 1 application of Lice Be Gone

½ cup coconut oil

20 drops tea tree essential oil

TO MAKE: Combine coconut oil and tea tree essential oil in a bowl. Mix well.

TO USE: Liberally add oil mixture to hair and scalp. Add enough to completely cover hair, then work into scalp well. Cover hair with plastic wrap and leave on for several hours or overnight. Remove plastic wrap and use a tight-tooth comb to comb hair from scalp to ends, removing lice and eggs. Repeat as necessary with a new application if lice remain.

SPIDER BE GONE

Spiders in your kitchen, bedroom, or living room are a thing of the past when you use this spray around your home. The strong smell of peppermint is one that spiders hate and will keep them away naturally!

YIELD: 1 cup

½ cup distilled water

½ cup vinegar

20 drops peppermint essential oil

TO MAKE: Combine all ingredients in a spray bottle. Shake well.

TO USE: Spray mixture around doors, windows, cracks, and crevices in and around your home.

TO STORE: Store indefinitely in spray bottle.

MICE BE GONE

Repelling mice is easy with this safe solution containing peppermint oil.

YIELD: 1 application of Mice Be Gone

1 cotton ball

1-2 drops peppermint essential oil

TO MAKE: Saturate cotton ball with peppermint essential oil.

TO USE: Place cotton ball where mice have been known to be. Remove every few days and replace with new cotton balls saturated with peppermint oil. You can place several cotton balls in a larger area if necessary.

DUST MITE BE GONE

Dust mites are small insects that lurk on your mattress and pillows. You may not realize they are there unless you look closely. Use this easy remedy to remove them safely! Lavender and tea tree essential oils are the perfect oils known to remove dust mites and freshen your space.

YIELD: 1 cup

1 cup baking soda

10 drops lavender essential oil

10 drops tea tree essential oil

TO MAKE: Combine baking soda and essential oils in a shaker jar or container. Mix well.

TO USE: Remove all bedding and sprinkle mixture over mattress and pillows. Allow to sit for several hours to remove dust mites and to remove odors and moisture. Vacuum thoroughly.

TO STORE: Store indefinitely in jar.

TIP Make your own shaker jar by poking holes in the metal lid of a Mason jar with a nail, or just use a spice jar, which already has holes in the top.

ON-THE-GO BED PURIFIER

Take this variation of a dust mite remover on the road for use when staying in hotels. The addition of cedarwood essential oil purifies and cleanses the spots where you'll be sleeping.

YIELD: 1 cup

1 cup distilled water

20 drops cedarwood essential oil

TO MAKE: Combine water and cedarwood essential oil in a spray bottle. Shake well.

TO USE: Spray bed linens thoroughly. Allow to dry.

TO STORE: Store indefinitely in spray bottle in a cool, dark place.

OUTDOOR SPRAY

Insects can be a bother when enjoying the outdoors. This nontoxic spray, which works great when sprayed on your clothes, is packed with the bug-repelling properties of tea tree, lavender, and rosemary essential oils and will help you stay bite-free.

YIELD: 1 cup

¾ cup distilled water

¼ cup witch hazel

10 drops tea tree essential oil

10 drops lavender essential oil

10 drops rosemary essential oil

TO MAKE: Combine all ingredients in a spray bottle. Shake well.

TO USE: Spray clothes with mixture before heading outdoors. Reapply every 15–30 minutes as needed.

TO STORE: Store indefinitely in spray bottle in a cool, dark place.

CITRONELLA CAMPING SPRAY

Take this outdoor camping spray that works best on exposed skin with you whenever you need to repel flies, mosquitoes, or other pests. Tea tree, citronella, and lavender essential oils are great options for this spray since they are well known for their bug-repelling properties.

YIELD: 1 cup

½ cup apple cider vinegar

½ cup witch hazel

10 drops tea tree essential oil

10 drops citronella essential oil

10 drops lavender essential oil

TO MAKE: Combine all ingredients in a spray bottle. Shake well.

TO USE: Spray mixture on all exposed skin, avoiding eyes and mouth. Reapply every 15–30 minutes as needed.

TO STORE: Store indefinitely in spray bottle.

FLYING INSECT OUTDOOR SPRAY

This easy DIY method for keeping away flying insects such as flies, mosquitoes, and gnats can be used again and again. Citronella, lavender, and peppermint essential oils will keep those pesky insects away!

YIELD: ¾ cup

½ cup vegetable oil

¼ cup apple cider vinegar

10 drops citronella essential oil

10 drops lavender essential oil

10 drops peppermint essential oil

TO MAKE: In a measuring cup, combine vegetable oil, apple cider vinegar, and essential oils.

TO USE: Add a cotton cloth to the top of a Mason jar and secure with outer ring from the Mason jar lid. Pour mixture into the Mason jar through the cloth. Place jar where you'd like to deter insects from being.

TO STORE: Add lid to cover cloth. Can be reused several times before essential oil mixture loses its scent and needs to be refreshed. Replace after 30 days.

MOTH BE GONE SACHETS

Repelling moths from your closets and drawers can be easy and smell good with these all-natural sachets made with herbs and essential oils like lavender, orange, and cedarwood, which are all known to keep moths away.

YIELD: 8–10 sachets

1 cup dried lavender flowers

20 drops lavender essential oil

10 drops orange essential oil

10 drops cedarwood essential oil

8–10 small muslin sachet bags (can be found at any craft store or online)

Twine or string

TO MAKE: Add dried lavender flowers to a large bowl. Mix in all essential oils. Add 1–2 tablespoons of mixture to each sachet bag and tie closed.

TO USE: Add scented sachets to drawers, closets, or other places moths are known to be. Freshen sachets with essential oil drops as needed.

TO STORE: Store sachets indefinitely in a sealed plastic bag or container.

INSECT BITE AND STING REMEDY

Try this Insect Bite and Sting Remedy to take away the pain fast! Lavender essential oil is the perfect choice due to its soothing properties.

YIELD: 1 application of Insect Bite and Sting Remedy

1 drop lavender essential oil

TO USE: Add 1 drop of lavender essential oil to bite or sting. Repeat as needed to remove pain.

BEE STING PASTE

When bees sting they can leave pain and swelling. Try this all-natural paste packed with the soothing properties of lavender and chamomile to take the pain and swelling away.

YIELD: 1 application of Bee Sting Paste

¼ cup baking soda

2 tablespoons distilled water

5 drops lavender essential oil

5 drops chamomile essential oil

TO MAKE: Combine baking soda, water, and essential oils in a small bowl. Mix well to make a paste.

TO USE: Make sure to remove the stinger before applying this mixture, being careful not to squeeze and break off the stinger. Scraping the stinger with a credit card or other straight object to remove it is best. Then apply mixture to area where sting occurred. Allow to dry on skin and then rinse off with cool water. Reapply if needed.

FRESH CITRUS AIR FRESHENER

This DIY air freshener is a simple way to freshen the air and remove odors without chemicals. Citrus essential oils are known for their cleansing properties and are the perfect ingredients in this easy spray!

YIELD: 1 cup

10 drops lemon essential oil

10 drops orange essential oil

1 cup distilled water

TO MAKE: Combine all ingredients in a spray bottle. Shake well.

TO USE: Mist the air with this spray wherever you'd like to freshen up. Can be used in kitchens, bathrooms, closets, or drawers.

TO STORE: Store indefinitely in spray bottle in a cool, dark place.

SPA FRESH ROOM FRESHENER SPRAY

The combination of lavender and lemon is perfect for providing a pleasant scent and removing odors from any room. This is always a winning combination for a comforting environment!

YIELD: 1 cup

¾ cup distilled water

¼ cup witch hazel

10 drops lavender essential oil

10 drops lemon essential oil

TO MAKE: Combine all ingredients in a spray bottle. Shake well.

TO USE: Spray into the air of any room, giving the bottle a shake before each use.

TO STORE: Store indefinitely in spray bottle in a cool, dark place.

PAINT SMELL NEUTRALIZER

Even paint that is low in volatile organic compounds (VOCs) can have a lingering smell. To remove the paint odor and ensure your freshly painted room smells as good as it looks, lemon essential oil is a great choice.

YIELD: 1 gallon paint

1 (15-milliliter) bottle lemon essential oil

1 gallon paint

TO USE: Add bottle of lemon essential oil to gallon of paint. Mix well.

TO STORE: Store paint can as usual.

PURIFYING ROOM SPRAY

This nontoxic Purifying Room Spray cleanses the air with ease! Combining tea tree and lemon essential oils with vinegar and rubbing alcohol ensures that you will remove odors easily.

YIELD: 1¾ cups

1 cup distilled water

½ cup vinegar

¼ cup rubbing alcohol or vodka

10 drops tea tree essential oil

10 drops lemon essential oil

TO MAKE: Combine water, vinegar, rubbing alcohol, and essential oils in a spray bottle. Shake well.

TO USE: Spray in the air or on surfaces to remove odors.

TO STORE: Store indefinitely in spray bottle.

TIP Undiluted essential oils should never be stored in plastic bottles, as they will break down the plastic and cause leaking. Glass is best. However, if you are diluting an oil and adding other ingredients to a recipe, a high-quality plastic bottle is just fine to use.

PLUG-IN AIR FRESHENER

Store-bought plug-in air fresheners are full of chemicals that you don't want to breathe in. Exchange the chemical freshener with an all-natural essential oil to freshen the air and remove any unpleasant odors.

YIELD: 1 air freshener

20-30 drops essential oils of choice (orange, lavender, lemongrass, etc.)

About ⅛ cup distilled water

1 empty commercial plug-in air freshener container

TO MAKE: Take the wick out of your old plug-in. Fill the container halfway with your chosen essential oils. Fill the remainder of the plug-in with distilled water, then replace the wick.

TO USE: Plug into wall outlet and use as normal.

REED DIFFUSER

Infuse your room with the scent of essential oils with this Reed Diffuser. By using the essential oil of your choice, you can create any mood you prefer!

YIELD: ¼ cup

¼ cup vegetable oil of choice (grapeseed, olive, almond, etc.)

20 drops essential oils of choice (lavender, lemon, peppermint, etc.)

4–6 (8") reed diffuser sticks or bamboo sticks

TO MAKE: Combine vegetable oil and your chosen essential oils in a glass bottle. Place diffuser sticks in the bottle and allow the oil mixture to travel up the sticks to diffuse into the air.

TO USE: Flip over the sticks from time to time to refresh the scents.

GEL AIR FRESHENER

Forget the chemical-filled gel air fresheners you can buy at the store. Instead, make your own Gel Air Freshener the natural way! Remove stinky odors and provide an uplifting atmosphere by using orange essential oil in this Gel Air Freshener.

YIELD: 1 gel air freshener

1 (8-ounce) glass jar

1 (1-ounce) packet floral hydration aqua beads (can be found at any craft store)

About ¾ cup distilled water

20 drops orange essential oil

TO MAKE: Fill the jar halfway with the floral hydration aqua beads. Add enough water to fill your jar to the top. Add orange essential oil to the jar and stir. Allow beads to soak up the water-oil mixture for several hours. Pour off extra water.

TO USE: Place your Gel Air Freshener in a small space—the bathroom, a closet, your desk area—to enjoy its fragrance.

TO STORE: Store covered in a cool, dark place for approximately 30 days.

POTPOURRI

This DIY Potpourri is as pretty as it is functional! Place it in a bowl in the living room or bathroom, or use it in sachets for the bedroom or car. The lavender and rosemary essential oils work hard to provide a clean, relaxing scent.

YIELD: 1 cup

1 small bouquet flowers of your choice (approximately 7-9 stems of flowers)

10 drops rosemary essential oil

10 drops lavender essential oil

TO MAKE: Preheat oven to 200°F. Remove the flowers from the stems and place on a baking sheet covered with parchment paper. Discard stems. Bake until flowers are dried out, approximately 2 hours. Remove from oven and set aside to cool. Once the flowers are cooled, add essential oils to the dried flowers on the baking sheet and mix gently.

TO USE: Add potpourri to bowls, vases, or sachets. Add a drop or two of essential oils to refresh scent as needed every week or so.

TO STORE: Store indefinitely in sealed container. Add the same essential oils to refresh scent or use a different essential oil scent every week or so.

WAX BURNER MELTS

Instead of filling the air with chemical fragrance, make your own Wax Burner Melts and add essential oils to cleanly freshen the air and remove odors. Add your favorite essential oils for whatever mood hits!

YIELD: 16 (1-ounce) Wax Burner Melts

1 (1-pound) block soy wax or beeswax, cut into small pieces (can be found at any craft store)

20 drops essential oils of choice

1-ounce silicone molds or ice cube trays

TO MAKE: Make a double boiler by simmering approximately 1 cup of water in a pot on the stove. Place a metal bowl slightly smaller than the pot over the water, then add wax to the bowl, stirring often until melted. Remove from heat and let cool. While the wax is still melted, add your chosen essential oils and stir well. Pour into molds and let harden for approximately 1 hour. When hardened completely, remove from molds.

TO USE: Add cubes to wax burner and use as normal.

TO STORE: Store wax cubes indefinitely in a covered container in a cool, dark place.

SCENTED LIGHT BULB

Easily bring an all-natural scent to your room by adding essential oils to your light bulbs! What's better than something that not only brightens but freshens, too?

YIELD: 1 application of Scented Light Bulb

1 drop essential oil of choice (lavender, lemon, and orange are great choices)

1 light bulb

TO MAKE: Add your chosen essential oil to the top of your light bulb.

TO USE: Screw the light bulb into the lamp and turn it on to add fragrance. Refresh as needed.

HOME AIR FILTER FRESHENER

Add fragrance to and remove odors from your home with this handy trick! By using a citrus oil, you'll remove odors and uplift your spirit at the same time.

YIELD: 1 application of Home Air Filter Freshener

3-4 drops citrus essential oil of choice (lemon, orange, and lime are great choices)

TO MAKE: Add your chosen essential oil to your air conditioner and furnace filters.

TO USE: Turn on your unit to fill your whole home with fragrance. Add more oil for a stronger scent or less for a subtler scent. Refresh as needed every couple of days.

CANDLE REFRESHER

Have a candle that seems to have lost its scent? Use this trick to refresh it the all-natural way without chemicals!

YIELD: 1 application of Candle Refresher

1-2 drops essential oil of choice

TO MAKE: Add your chosen essential oil to the top of your candle.

TO USE: Burn the candle as normal. Add more essential oil each time you are going to use your candle to keep the fragrance fresh.

TO STORE: Store as normal and refresh each time you light your candle.

CITRONELLA CANDLE

Citronella is known to keep insects away. Use this essential oil to make your own outdoor candle the all-natural way without harmful chemicals.

YIELD: 2 Citronella Candles

2 (6") candle wicks (can be found at any craft store)

2 (½-pint) Mason jars

Glue gun and hot glue

2 wooden popsicle sticks

1 (1-pound) block soy wax or beeswax

20 drops citronella essential oil

TO MAKE: Prepare candleholder by gluing a wick to the inside bottom of each Mason jar with your glue gun. Wrap the top end of each wick around a popsicle stick and lay stick across the top of the jar to keep it in place. Make a double boiler by simmering 1 cup of water in a pot on the stove. Place a metal bowl slightly smaller than the pot over the water, then add wax to the bowl. Stir wax until melted. Remove from heat and add citronella oil to melted wax. Stir well. Add melted wax to candle jars evenly, adjusting wicks if needed once the liquid is completely poured in. Allow to harden for 4–6 hours or longer if needed. Trim wick to ¼" tall before lighting.

TO USE: Burn as normal.

TO STORE: Store indefinitely in a cool, dark location.

CLOTHES DRAWER FRESHENER

Keep clothes smelling fresh and clean longer with essential oils. There's no need to reach for expensive store-bought sprays and sachets when you can do it yourself at home for next to nothing! Lavender essential oil is a great choice because its wonderful fragrance is long-lasting.

YIELD: 1 Clothes Drawer Freshener

1 cotton ball

2-3 drops lavender essential oil

TO MAKE: Saturate cotton ball with lavender essential oil, then allow to dry.

TO USE: Place 1 cotton ball in each clothes drawer to keep clothes smelling fresh.

STINKY SHOE REFRESHER

Don't throw out those stinky shoes; use this trick to remove odors and keep them fresh. Lemon essential oil is great for removing odors and leaving a clean scent.

YIELD: 1 Stinky Shoe Refresher

1 pair old socks or nylon pantyhose

¼ cup baking soda

10 drops lemon essential oil

6" twine or string

TO MAKE: Cut off the foot portions of the pair of old socks or pantyhose. Add ⅛ cup baking soda and 5 drops lemon essential oil to the toe area of each. Tie closed with twine or string.

TO USE: Add to shoes overnight or until you wear them again. Add 5 drops of lemon essential oil to the baking soda mixture inside each refresher before each use to keep the fragrance fresh.

HOMEMADE GOO REMOVER

This Homemade Goo Remover gets its extra grime-fighting power from the lemon essential oil. It's better than any commercial product you may have tried—guaranteed!

YIELD: 1 cup

½ cup baking soda

½ cup coconut oil

10 drops lemon essential oil

TO MAKE: Combine all ingredients in a bowl. Mix well to make a paste.

TO USE: Apply paste mixture to adhesive remaining from stickers or labels, or any other sticky substance. Let sit for 10–15 minutes and rub off. Rinse under warm water to help remove paste and remaining adhesive.

TO STORE: Store indefinitely in a small glass jar with a lid in a cool, dark place.

CHAPTER 3

Floors, Walls, and Other Surfaces

To get your home truly clean, start at the top and work your way down! This chapter is filled with all-natural, chemical-free solutions to clean your floors, walls, and other surfaces in your home with the power of essential oils. Essential oils are natural purifiers, which make them the perfect additions to your cleaning products. Tea tree, lemon, orange, eucalyptus, and pine essential oils will cut through grease and grime and leave your home smelling fresh and clean without irritating your eyes and lungs like commercial cleaning products can. Throughout this chapter, you'll find a variety of different options for cleaning your carpets, floors, and walls. Pick your favorite and change up the essential oils if you want—it's up to you! That's the beauty of making your own cleaning products at home: You are in control of what goes in. The next time you need to get your floors or walls sparkling clean or need to cleanse a hard surface, just reach for one of these nontoxic cleaners that you can feel good about using in your home.

NATURAL CARPET CLEANER

This all-natural carpet cleaner—which can be used in a carpet cleaner machine or to spot-clean—is gentle on your carpet and your body. The cleaning powers of vinegar, borax, and tea tree essential oil team up to create the perfect combination of stain remover and deodorizer.

YIELD: 1 gallon

½ gallon distilled water

½ gallon white vinegar

¼ cup borax

25-30 drops tea tree essential oil

TO MAKE: Combine all ingredients in a large bucket or 1-gallon container. Mix well.

TO USE: Add as much of the mixture as needed to the solution area of your carpet cleaner machine. Use as directed. Or, if spot-cleaning, add some of this solution to a spray bottle and spray solution onto carpet, rubbing in with a clean cloth.

TO STORE: Store indefinitely in 1-gallon container.

TEA TREE AND LEMON CARPET CLEANER SOLUTION

There's no need to overpay for chemical-filled carpet cleaner machine solutions! This all-natural solution is perfect for getting carpets extra clean, as it removes dirt and grime while purifying with tea tree and lemon essential oils, some of the strongest purifying oils available. This borax-free recipe is very clean and green. No need to worry about chemicals here!

YIELD: 2 cups, or 1 application of Tea Tree and Lemon Carpet Cleaner Solution

1 cup distilled water

1 cup vinegar

1 tablespoon liquid Castile soap

20 drops tea tree essential oil

10 drops lemon essential oil

TO MAKE: Combine water, vinegar, soap, and essential oils in a small plastic container. Mix together carefully. Add entire batch to the solution area of your carpet cleaner machine.

TO USE: Clean carpet as usual with machine, being careful to not oversaturate the carpet.

ORANGE FOAMING CARPET SHAMPOO

Try this foaming carpet soap in high-traffic areas that need a little extra attention. Orange essential oil will help to remove any stains and cut through grime with ease.

YIELD: 5 cups, or 1 application of Orange Foaming Carpet Shampoo

4 cups warm distilled water

1 cup liquid Castile soap

20 drops orange essential oil

TO MAKE: Combine all ingredients in a large plastic container or bucket. Using an immersion blender, blend solution until foam forms.

TO USE: Apply solution to carpet. Scrub well. Allow to dry and vacuum.

VARIATION

If you don't have an immersion blender, just add small amounts of the mixture to a blender and "foam" it up.

LEMON CARPET STAIN REMOVER

Spills can happen! Use this carpet stain remover to get your carpet back to normal with the cleaning power of lemon essential oil.

YIELD: 1 cup, or 1 application of Lemon Carpet Stain Remover

1 cup vinegar

10 drops lemon essential oil

¼ cup baking soda

TO MAKE: Combine vinegar and lemon essential oil in a measuring cup or bottle. Mix well.

TO USE: Sprinkle enough baking soda over stain to cover. Pour mixture over stain as needed. The baking soda will bubble up. Let dry. Vacuum. This may take a day or so to dry, depending on your stain and the thickness of your carpet.

LAVENDER CARPET FRESHENER

Everyone loves the smell of lavender, and this carpet freshener is a great way to bring this lasting scent into your home. Use this carpet freshener to remove odors and purify with the power of lavender essential oil.

YIELD: 1 cup

1 cup baking soda

10-15 drops lavender essential oil

TO MAKE: Combine baking soda and lavender essential oil in a small glass Mason jar or spice container. Stir well to combine. Poke holes in the metal Mason jar lid and cover, or cover with spice container lid.

TO USE: Sprinkle mixture over carpet. Let sit for 10 minutes before vacuuming.

TO STORE: Store indefinitely in jar or container.

VACUUM FRESHENER

Perk up your vacuuming with the addition of peppermint and orange essential oils while you remove airborne odors. These essential oils will freshen your vacuum and the air in the room, making your room smell fresh and clean—naturally.

YIELD: 1 application of Vacuum Freshener

4 drops peppermint essential oil

4 drops orange essential oil

TO MAKE: Add essential oils to vacuum filter, or add to a small (2" square) piece of paper.

TO USE: Vacuum as normal, or vacuum up the paper, then vacuum as normal.

FRESH ORANGE FLOOR CLEANER

Making your kitchen floor shine is easy with this homemade solution! The orange essential oil in this recipe cuts through grease and grime and leaves your room smelling fresh and clean.

YIELD: 1 application of Fresh Orange Floor Cleaner

1 gallon water

½ cup vinegar

20 drops orange essential oil

TO MAKE: Combine all ingredients in a 2-gallon (or larger) bucket. Mix well.

TO USE: Using a mop, clean floor as usual.

TIP Try using a mop that has the cleaning solution container on the handle, such as the Libman Freedom Spray Mop. You spray the cleaner on the floor as you go and mop it up with the reusable mop pads that can be thrown into the washer. This great green tip will save you time and money!

WOOD FLOOR CLEANER

Cleaning your wood floors doesn't require expensive solutions. Try this citrus-powered Wood Floor Cleaner that cleans and shines at the same time!

YIELD: 2¼ cups

2 cups distilled water

¼ cup vinegar

10 drops lemon essential oil

10 drops orange essential oil

TO MAKE: Combine all ingredients in a spray bottle. Shake well.

TO USE: Spray a small amount onto floors and mop as usual with a clean microfiber or reusable cloth mop. Be careful not to oversaturate the mop with the spray.

TO STORE: Store indefinitely in spray bottle.

CONDITIONING WOOD FLOOR CLEANER

Clean and condition your floors with this all-natural cleaner that will leave a nice lemon scent as it purifies and shines your wood floors. What could be better than conditioning your wood with lemon and olive oils?

YIELD: 1 application of Conditioning Wood Floor Cleaner

1 gallon warm water

½ cup olive oil

½ cup lemon juice

20 drops lemon essential oil

TO MAKE: Combine all ingredients in a large bucket. Mix well.

TO USE: Mop floors as normal. No need to rinse.

FLOOR WAX REMOVER

Cleaning excess wax off floors can be hard to do, even with commercial cleaners. But with lemon essential oil, this all-natural version is safe and effective. Lemon essential oil cuts through the sticky wax and leaves a clean, fresh scent behind!

YIELD: 5 cups, or 1 application of Floor Wax Remover

4 cups water

1 cup vinegar

2 tablespoons liquid Castile soap

20 drops lemon essential oil

TO MAKE: Combine all ingredients in a small bucket and mix well.

TO USE: Wet a mop or a cloth with the solution, then apply to a small section of floor. Scrub with mop or a bristle brush. Wipe dry with a clean cloth or towel before moving on to another section.

WOOD FLOOR POLISHER

Cleaning your hardwood floors is simple with this all-natural cleaner that relies on the shine power of lemon essential oil and the cleansing properties of tea tree essential oil to work its magic. You'll have beautiful floors in no time!

YIELD: 1 application of Wood Floor Polisher

1 gallon warm water

½ cup olive oil

20 drops lemon essential oil

20 drops tea tree essential oil

TO MAKE: Combine all ingredients in a large bucket or spray-mop container.

TO USE: Using a microfiber mop, mop as usual. No need to rinse.

TILE FLOOR CLEANER

Cleaning your tile floors is a breeze with this nontoxic cleaning solution! The tea tree and lemon essential oils cut through dirt and grime with ease and leave a clean, fresh scent!

YIELD: 1 gallon, or 1 application of Tile Floor Cleaner

1 gallon hot water

¼ cup borax

20 drops tea tree essential oil

20 drops lemon essential oil

TO MAKE: Combine water and borax in a large bucket. Mix well. Add in essential oils.

TO USE: Mop as normal. No need to rinse.

LAMINATE FLOOR CLEANER

Laminate floors are notorious for being hard to get clean without leaving water spots and streaks. Try this floor cleaner that is sure to leave your floors streak-free and clean. With the addition of lavender essential oil, this cleaner is guaranteed to leave a nice scent in your home, too!

YIELD: 1½ cups

½ cup vinegar

½ cup distilled water

½ cup rubbing alcohol

5 drops lavender essential oil

TO MAKE: Combine all ingredients in a large spray bottle. Shake well.

TO USE: Lightly spray a small section of floor with mixture and mop well using a microfiber mop. Repeat until entire floor is clean, making sure not to get the floor sections too wet each time. No need to rinse.

TO STORE: Store indefinitely in spray bottle.

VINYL FLOOR CLEANER

Vinyl floors can get dirty and grimy pretty quick, but don't fret! This easy Vinyl Floor Cleaner made without chemicals will clean your room to a shine in no time! Lemon and peppermint essential oils will help cut through dirt, purify your floors, and leave a fresh, clean scent!

YIELD: 1 application of Vinyl Floor Cleaner

1 gallon warm water

½ cup vinegar

¼ cup borax

10 drops lemon essential oil

10 drops peppermint essential oil

TO MAKE: Combine all ingredients in a large bucket. Mix well.

TO USE: Mop as usual. No need to rinse.

ALCOHOL-FREE LEMON WINDOW AND GLASS CLEANER

Making your own window and glass cleaner is a breeze! This streak-free cleaner will degrease and degrime without chemicals, leaving your room smelling fresh and clean.

YIELD: 1¼ cups

1 cup distilled water

¼ cup vinegar

10–12 drops lemon or lime essential oil

TO MAKE: Combine all ingredients in a spray bottle. Shake well.

TO USE: Spray on window or glass and wipe with a lint-free cloth or newspaper.

TO STORE: Store indefinitely in glass bottle in a cool, dark place to preserve essential oil properties. Shake bottle prior to each use to mix ingredients.

MULTISURFACE CLEANER

Good on windows, glass, counters, sinks, and more, this go-to Multisurface Cleaner will quickly become your favorite household cleaner. Lemon and tea tree essential oils clean and remove odors and grime, making this a great all-surface cleaner.

YIELD: 2 cups

1 cup distilled water

1 cup vinegar

20 drops lemon essential oil

20 drops tea tree essential oil

TO MAKE: Combine all ingredients in a spray bottle. Shake well.

TO USE: Spray on surface and wipe clean with a microfiber cloth or paper towel.

TO STORE: Store indefinitely in spray bottle in a cool, dark place. Shake well before each use.

WALLPAPER REMOVER

Removing wallpaper can be a pain and expensive with store-bought solutions, but this Wallpaper Remover is easy on your wallet and your home! Lemon essential oil is perfect for removing sticky glue; plus, it removes any old odors that the glue may have left behind.

YIELD: 2 cups, or 1 application of Wallpaper Remover

1 cup very hot water

1 cup vinegar

30 drops lemon essential oil

TO MAKE: Combine all ingredients in a spray bottle and shake well.

TO USE: Saturate one small section of wallpaper at a time. Allow to sit for 5–10 minutes, then scrape off with a plastic putty knife. If necessary, go back over the walls with this solution and wipe down with a clean cloth to remove any remaining glue.

CITRUS WALL AND BASEBOARD CLEANER

Walls and baseboards can get dusty and dirty without you even realizing it. Easily clean off dust and grime with this citrusy cleaner. Lemon and orange essential oils are also the perfect choice for purifying and deodorizing.

YIELD: 2 cups, or 1 application of Citrus Wall and Baseboard Cleaner

1½ cups water

½ cup vinegar

1 tablespoon liquid Castile soap

10 drops lemon essential oil

10 drops orange essential oil

TO MAKE: Combine all ingredients in a spray bottle. Shake well.

TO USE: Spray down walls and baseboards with mixture. Wipe well with a clean sponge or microfiber cloth. Rinse out sponge or cloth with clean water, then wipe the solution off the surfaces to make sure the walls and baseboards are clean.

WALL CLEANER

Use this Wall Cleaner for your toughest jobs. Remove dirt, dust, grime, and odors with this all-natural cleaning solution that includes tea tree and pine essential oils to get the dirtiest of walls clean.

YIELD: 1 application of Wall Cleaner

2 gallons hot water

2 cups vinegar

2 cups borax

20 drops tea tree essential oil

20 drops pine essential oil

TO MAKE: Combine water, vinegar, and borax in a large bucket. Mix well. Add in essential oils.

TO USE: Soak a lint-free cloth with mixture and wipe down walls from top to bottom. For tough jobs, use a scrubbing sponge, rinsing often. When water is dirty, discard and refill bucket with fresh cleaning mixture.

DUST CLOTHS

Homemade dust cloths are easy and economical to make, and good for the environment! Use these essential oil-soaked cloths to clean and shine anything, from tabletops to side tables to over the doorways. You'll leave behind a fresh, clean scent as well.

YIELD: 2 cups

1 cup distilled water

1 cup vinegar

1 tablespoon olive oil

20 drops lemon essential oil

10 drops peppermint essential oil

TO MAKE: Combine all ingredients in a large airtight jar or container. Add several cut-up T-shirts or washcloths to the mixture. Allow them to soak up the solution until thoroughly wet. Next, take the cloths out of the jar and wring them out until slightly damp. Discard remaining solution. Fold cloths, place back in airtight jar, and close until needed.

TO USE: Remove dust cloth from jar and use to wipe down any dusty surfaces. Launder for next use.

TO STORE: Store indefinitely in closed airtight jar in a cool, dark place.

LEMON ROSEMARY DUSTING WIPES

Get your house dust-free and smelling great with these Lemon Rosemary Dusting Wipes. This easy, nontoxic recipe will rid your home of dirt and dust while also providing a purified surface, thanks to the addition of lemon and rosemary essential oils.

YIELD: 40 wipes

3 cups distilled water

1 cup vinegar

1 tablespoon liquid Castile soap

2 tablespoons olive oil

10 drops lemon essential oil

10 drops rosemary essential oil

40 (4" × 4") cotton or cloth squares

TO MAKE: Combine all ingredients except cotton squares in a large container with a lid. Add several of the cotton squares to the mixture. Allow them to soak well.

TO USE: Whenever you need to clean or dust a surface, remove one of the cotton squares and squeeze out the excess mixture. Use to wipe down dusty surfaces. After each use, launder and return clean cloth to container.

TO STORE: Store indefinitely in container.

LEMON WOOD POLISH

Forget the aerosol can of chemical wood polish. Instead, try this all-natural version that will leave your wood clean and shining in no time! Lemon essential oil is the perfect addition to this polish since it brings natural nourishing properties to all types of wood.

YIELD: ¼ cup

¼ cup olive oil

10 drops lemon essential oil

TO MAKE: Combine olive oil and lemon essential oil in a bowl or small squeeze bottle.

TO USE: Place a small amount of mixture on a lint-free cloth. Gently buff wood furniture until polish is rubbed in and wood looks clean.

TO STORE: Store indefinitely in small bottle in a cool, dark place.

WOOD CLEANER

Use this cleaner in your home to clean all of your wood surfaces, from tables and chairs to dressers and side tables. You can feel good about using this nontoxic, nourishing cleaner with lemon essential oil to get those wood surfaces shining and clean!

YIELD: 2 cups

1 cup distilled water

½ cup vinegar

½ cup olive oil

20 drops lemon essential oil

TO MAKE: Combine all ingredients in a large spray bottle. Shake well.

TO USE: Lightly spray surfaces to be cleaned. Wipe with a damp, lint-free cloth. Allow to air-dry.

TO STORE: Store indefinitely in spray bottle.

FURNITURE SCRATCH FILLER

Don't pull out the heavy stains when wood furniture gets scratched. Use this all-natural solution with orange essential oil to get it back to normal and shiny clean!

YIELD: 1 cup

½ cup olive oil

½ cup vinegar

20 drops orange essential oil

TO MAKE: Combine all ingredients in a bowl. Mix well.

TO USE: Dip a lint-free cloth in mixture. Rub onto furniture until the scratch is covered and the mixture is rubbed in.

TO STORE: Store indefinitely in a covered container.

WOOD PANELING CLEANER

With this all-natural cleaning solution, you can keep your wood paneling clean and looking great. The lemon and orange essential oils in this cleaner condition your wood and remove odors the natural way!

YIELD: 2 gallons, or 1 application of Wood Paneling Cleaner

2 gallons hot water

1 cup vinegar

½ cup olive oil

½ cup liquid Castile soap

20 drops lemon essential oil

20 drops orange essential oil

TO MAKE: Add water to a large bucket. Add vinegar, olive oil, soap, and essential oils. Mix well.

TO USE: Dip a lint-free cloth into the solution and wipe down walls from top to bottom, ending with baseboards.

LEATHER CLEANER

To revitalize leather, try this olive oil-based cleaner with the nourishing and conditioning power of lemon to make leather as good as new!

YIELD: 1¼ cups

½ cup olive oil

¾ cup vinegar

10 drops lemon
essential oil

TO MAKE: Combine all ingredients in a spray bottle. Shake well.

TO USE: Spray cleaner on a lint-free cloth or directly onto furniture. Wipe clean.

TO STORE: Store indefinitely in spray bottle.

TEA TREE MATTRESS CLEANER

It's tough to remember that your mattress needs to be cleaned on a regular basis. Fortunately, this often overlooked chore is easy to do with this all-natural mattress cleaner! Tea tree essential oil removes odors and dirt with its cleansing and purifying properties.

YIELD: 2 cups, or 1 application of Tea Tree Mattress Cleaner

2 cups baking soda

10 drops tea tree essential oil

TO MAKE: Combine baking soda and tea tree essential oil in a jar. Mix well.

TO USE: Remove all bedding and wash in hottest possible water. Sprinkle mixture over bare mattress. Leave on for about an hour to draw out moisture and odor and remove dust and dirt. Vacuum thoroughly.

YOGA MAT CLEANER

To get your yoga mat odor- and grime-free, use this DIY cleaner that purifies and cleanses with tea tree and lavender essential oils.

YIELD: 1 cup

¾ cup distilled water

¼ cup witch hazel

5 drops tea tree essential oil

5 drops lavender essential oil

TO MAKE: Combine all ingredients in a large measuring cup. Mix well, then pour into a spray bottle.

TO USE: Spray on yoga mat after use. Wipe clean with a dry cloth. Let air-dry before rolling back up.

TO STORE: Store indefinitely in spray bottle.

FLOOR SCUFF REMOVER

Remove floor scuffs with lemon essential oil and this one trick! Lemon is known to break down stains and remove any greasy messes, so it's perfect for floor scuffs. Add this to a tennis ball, an item that's great for getting rid of those unsightly marks.

YIELD: 1 application of Floor Scuff Remover

1 drop lemon essential oil

1 tennis ball

TO MAKE: Place 1 drop of lemon essential oil on a scuff on the floor.

TO USE: Using a tennis ball, rub in the essential oil until the scuff has disappeared.

KEYBOARD CLEANER

Keep your keyboard clean with this gentle keyboard cleaning solution. This cleaner will be easy on your keyboard while getting rid of dirt and grime with the cleansing properties of tea tree essential oil.

YIELD: ½ cup

¼ cup rubbing alcohol

¼ cup vinegar

10 drops tea tree essential oil

TO MAKE: Combine all ingredients in a small spray bottle

TO USE: Spray a very small amount of cleaner onto a microfiber cloth, being careful not to get cloth too wet. Carefully wipe keyboard and keys, removing dust and grime. Repeat as necessary.

TO STORE: Store indefinitely in small spray bottle.

ELECTRONIC SCREEN CLEANER

Purify and keep your electronic screens clean with this gentle cleaner with tea tree essential oil.

YIELD: ¼ cup

¼ cup vinegar

10 drops tea tree essential oil

TO MAKE: Combine vinegar and tea tree essential oil in a bottle with a fine-mist spray top. Shake well.

TO USE: Turn off electronics before cleaning. Lightly mist a lint-free cloth with mixture and use the cloth to wipe electronics clean.

TO STORE: Store indefinitely in spray bottle.

CELL PHONE CLEANER

Cell phones can get dirty, grimy, and full of who knows what else! Get yours super clean with this easy Cell Phone Cleaner with tea tree essential oil.

YIELD: ½ cup

¼ cup vinegar

¼ cup vodka

10 drops tea tree essential oil

TO MAKE: Combine all ingredients in a spray bottle with a fine-mist spray top. Shake well.

TO USE: Lightly mist a lint-free cloth with mixture and use it to wipe clean cell phone.

TO STORE: Store indefinitely in spray bottle.

CHAPTER 4

Kitchen

Give your kitchen a makeover with the all-natural dish soap, dishwasher detergents, counter cleaner, cutting board cleaner, trashcan deodorizer, and more found in this chapter! The last place you want to use chemicals is in your kitchen, where you are at risk of ingesting who knows what. Here you'll learn how to get rid of all of your chemical-filled products and exchange them for new green, clean products that you make yourself. With the purifying power of lemon, the grease-cutting ability of orange, and the cleansing properties of lavender and tea tree, you can clean just about anything safely. Add in vinegar, baking soda, salt, and liquid Castile soap and you have a winning combination of cleaners to use with confidence! To mix up these cleaners, you'll need a plastic or glass spray bottle (remember, glass is best), a bowl or a bucket, plus your normal everyday kitchen items like measuring spoons and measuring cups. Don't worry about these items not being safe to use after you've made these cleaners. Just wash them as normal after you're done. There are no chemicals to worry about here!

ALL-PURPOSE COUNTER CLEANER

This All-Purpose Counter Cleaner is wonderful for all kinds of kitchen messes. Tea tree essential oil will cleanse and purify your surface without all the chemicals and ingredients you can't pronounce found in commercial cleaners.

YIELD: 1 cup

¾ cup distilled water

¼ cup vinegar

20–30 drops tea tree essential oil

TO MAKE: Combine all ingredients in a spray bottle. Shake well.

TO USE: Spray counters with mixture. Wipe clean with a damp cloth.

TO STORE: Store indefinitely in spray bottle.

ALL-PURPOSE CITRUS KITCHEN CLEANER

Citrus oils are the perfect essential oils for any job—big or small—in the kitchen. They cut through grease, purify surfaces, remove odors, and leave a clean, fresh scent!

YIELD: 1 cup

½ cup vinegar

½ cup distilled water

2 tablespoons rubbing alcohol

5 drops lemon essential oil

5 drops orange essential oil

5 drops lime essential oil

TO MAKE: Combine all ingredients in a spray bottle. Shake well.

TO USE: Spray on kitchen surfaces. Wipe clean.

TO STORE: Store indefinitely in spray bottle in a cool, dark place.

TIP | Any combination of essential oils can be used in this recipe. Tea tree, eucalyptus, and pine work well!

LEMON MICROWAVE CLEANER

Forget scrubbing! Lemon essential oil cuts through grease, dirt, and grime and removes odors. This easy-to-make cleaner will have your microwave clean and lemony fresh in no time.

YIELD: 1 application of Lemon Microwave Cleaner

1 cup water

10 drops lemon essential oil

TO MAKE: Combine water and lemon essential oil in a mug. Mix well.

TO USE: Place mug in microwave and cook on high for 2 minutes. Let sit in microwave for 5 minutes. Open door and wipe the entire inside and door with a wet cloth. Repeat as needed until clean.

DISHWASHER CLEANER

Cleaning your dishwasher couldn't be easier with this simple recipe. Here, your favorite hardworking essential oils such as lemon, orange, or lime work hard to get the inside of your dishwasher clean, purified, and sparkling clean.

YIELD: 1 application of Dishwasher Cleaner

1 cup vinegar

10 drops essential oil of choice (lemon, lime, and orange are great choices)

TO MAKE: Combine vinegar and your chosen essential oil in a dishwasher-safe cup. Mix well.

TO USE: Place cup with mixture on the top rack of your empty dishwasher. Turn on dishwasher and allow vinegar mixture to go to work.

REFRIGERATOR CLEANER

There's no need to use chemicals near your food. Using a food-safe cleaner in your refrigerator is a much better idea. This simple vinegar, water, and lemon essential oil cleaner is guaranteed to leave your refrigerator clean and odor-free!

**YIELD: 1 cup, or
1 application of
Refrigerator Cleaner**

½ cup vinegar

½ cup hot water

10 drops lemon
essential oil

TO MAKE: Combine all ingredients in a spray bottle or bucket.

TO USE: While water is still hot, wet a cloth with the solution and wipe down the inside of refrigerator thoroughly. No need to rinse!

STOVETOP CLEANER PASTE

Keeping your stovetop clean is a breeze with this stovetop cleaner. Remove grime and grease easily with this simple paste cleaner kicked up a notch with orange essential oil.

**YIELD: 1 application of
Stovetop Cleaner Paste**

½ cup baking soda

3 tablespoons water

10 drops orange
essential oil

TO MAKE: In a bowl, combine baking soda, water, and orange essential oil. Mix well to make a paste. If desired, add a little more water to make it the consistency you'd like.

TO USE: Using a cloth, wipe the paste all over the stovetop and let sit for 5 minutes. Come back and scrub clean with a soft cloth, rinsing your cloth in clean water as you go.

GLASS STOVETOP CLEANER

Water stains and burned-on food can make your glass stove-top unsightly. Use this easy recipe that combines Castile soap and orange essential oil to get your stovetop sparkling clean without harsh abrasives.

YIELD: 2 cups, or 1 application of Glass Stovetop Cleaner

2 cups hot water

2 tablespoons liquid Castile soap

1 cup baking soda

10 drops orange essential oil

TO MAKE: Combine hot water and soap in a bowl. Mix well. Then combine baking soda and orange essential oil in another bowl. Mix well.

TO USE: Sprinkle baking-soda mixture over entire stovetop. Dip a large dishtowel into the soapy water. Squeeze out a small amount of the water, leaving the towel mostly wet. Place towel over baking-soda mixture on stovetop. Allow to sit for 10 minutes, then use dishtowel to scrub the stovetop clean. Use fresh water to clean to a shine.

STAINLESS STEEL CLEANER

No need to worry about dirt and fingerprints on your stainless steel appliances! This Stainless Steel Cleaner is easy to whip up and safe for the whole family, and it smells amazing. The lemon essential oil is perfect for cutting right through whatever comes its way.

YIELD: ½ cup

¼ cup vinegar

¼ cup rubbing alcohol

10 drops lemon essential oil

TO MAKE: Combine all ingredients in a spray bottle. Shake well.

TO USE: Spray on stainless steel appliances and wipe clean with a lint-free cloth or paper towels.

TO STORE: Store indefinitely in spray bottle.

LEMON GARBAGE DISPOSAL FRESHENER

Freshening and cleaning your stinky garbage disposal the all-natural way is easy with these DIY lemon disposal freshener tabs. Lemon essential oil has the power to cut through grease and grime and remove odors.

YIELD: 36 tabs

2 cups baking soda

1 cup salt

½ cup distilled water

¼ cup liquid Castile soap

20 drops lemon essential oil

TO MAKE: In a large bowl, combine the baking soda and salt. Add in the water, soap, and lemon essential oil. Mix well. Using a small cookie scoop, scoop out tabs onto a cookie sheet covered in parchment paper. Leave out uncovered to harden overnight.

TO USE: Add 1 tab to garbage disposal, turn on water, and start disposal.

TO STORE: Store indefinitely in a closed jar or container in a cool, dark place.

COFFEE MAKER CLEANER

You may not think to clean your coffee maker, but it's easy to do and makes a big difference in how your machine works. Lemon essential oil makes this recipe work even harder and clean even deeper than a more basic recipe.

YIELD: 1 application of Coffee Maker Cleaner

Water (half the coffee pot)

Vinegar (half the coffee pot)

5 drops lemon essential oil

TO MAKE: Fill coffee pot with half water and half vinegar. Add lemon essential oil and stir to combine.

TO USE: Run mixture through your coffee maker as usual. Then run several cycles with clean water until the vinegar smell dissipates.

GLASS SPOT REMOVER

Nobody likes spots on their drinking glasses. Use this rinse with lemon essential oil to remove spots in no time!

YIELD: 1 gallon, or 1 application of Glass Spot Remover

½ gallon hot distilled water

½ gallon vinegar

10 drops lemon essential oil

TO MAKE: Fill your sink with hot water and vinegar. Add lemon essential oil and stir to combine.

TO USE: Add glasses to water and allow to sit for an hour. Remove from water and rinse well.

KITCHEN GROUT CLEANER

Dirt can get stuck in grout and make your once bright grout lines look dingy and dark, which is not what you want in your clean kitchen. This nonchemical grout cleaner works like a charm every time! Tea tree and lemon essential oils clean, brighten, and get rid of any grime caused by the cooking process.

YIELD: 7¼ cups, or 1 application of Kitchen Grout Cleaner

7 cups hot water

¼ cup baking soda

¼ cup vinegar

10 drops tea tree essential oil

10 drops lemon essential oil

TO MAKE: Combine all ingredients in a bucket. Mix well.

TO USE: Use a dishcloth to add cleaning mixture to grout lines. Allow to sit for several minutes. Use a scrub brush and scrub grout lines. Rinse with fresh water.

GRANITE CLEANER

Get your granite looking brand new with this DIY Granite Cleaner! The orange essential oil used in this recipe will work hard to get it shiny and clean at the same time.

YIELD: 2½ cups

½ cup rubbing alcohol

2 cups distilled water

1 tablespoon liquid Castile soap

10 drops orange essential oil

TO MAKE: Combine all ingredients in a large spray bottle. Shake well.

TO USE: Spray on granite. Wipe clean with a damp dishcloth.

TO STORE: Store indefinitely in spray bottle.

CABINET CLEANER

Cabinets can get sticky and dirty from cooking in the kitchen. Use this all-natural cleaner with grease-cutting eucalyptus and lemon essential oils to get them looking as good as new!

YIELD: 6 cups, or 1 application of Cabinet Cleaner

4 cups hot water

2 cups vinegar

½ cup liquid Castile soap

5 drops eucalyptus essential oil

10 drops lemon essential oil

TO MAKE: Combine all ingredients in a bowl or bucket. Mix well.

TO USE: Dip a clean dishtowel in solution and wipe on cabinets. Clean until grime and grease are gone. Rinse dishtowel in mixture as needed and wring out before using.

LAVENDER DISH SOAP

Doing dishes doesn't have to be a chore! The lavender essential oil in this recipe creates a pleasing aroma and cleanse at the same time.

YIELD: 1½ cups

1 cup liquid Castile soap

¼ cup distilled water

2 teaspoons vegetable glycerin

10 drops lavender essential oil

TO MAKE: Combine all ingredients in an empty dish soap bottle, a glass bottle with a liquid pour spout, or a squeeze bottle. Shake gently.

TO USE: Use as normal for washing dishes by hand.

TO STORE: Store indefinitely in bottle.

CITRUS LIQUID DISHWASHER DETERGENT

Why buy liquid dishwasher detergent for a high price when you can make your own and do it the all-natural way? In this recipe, which is sure to become one of your favorites, the cleaning power of orange and lemon essential oils will leave your dishes clean and spot-free!

YIELD: 2½ cups

2 cups liquid Castile soap

½ cup distilled water

10 drops lemon essential oil

10 drops orange essential oil

TO MAKE: Combine all ingredients in a squeeze bottle. Shake well.

TO USE: Add 1–2 tablespoons to dishwasher detergent cup. Run as normal.

TO STORE: Store indefinitely in squeeze bottle.

TIP Add vinegar to rinse-agent cup in your dishwasher instead of commercial rinse aid to get dishes sparkling clean naturally.

ORANGE DISHWASHER DETERGENT TABLETS

These dishwasher detergent tablets are all-natural, smell great, and get your dishes super clean without added chemicals. Orange essential oil removes stuck-on food and is purifying, which means that your dishes come out of your dishwasher extra clean!

YIELD: 16 tablets

1 cup baking soda

1 cup washing soda, such as Arm & Hammer (can be found in the laundry aisle)

¼ cup salt

¼ cup citric acid

¼ cup vinegar

10 drops orange essential oil

Ice cube trays

TO MAKE: In a large bowl, combine baking soda, washing soda, salt, and citric acid. Stir to combine. Add in vinegar and orange essential oil. It will bubble up for a minute. Once it's done bubbling, add the mixture to ice cube trays and pack down with the back of a spoon or your fingers. Allow to dry uncovered on the counter overnight before removing from the trays and adding to an airtight container or jar.

TO USE: Add 1 tablet to the dishwasher detergent dispenser before running the dishwasher.

TO STORE: Store indefinitely in airtight container in a cool, dark place.

POWDERED DISHWASHER DETERGENT

Making your own Powdered Dishwasher Detergent will leave your dishes chemical-free and save you money in the process! Lemon essential oil adds extra cleaning power and removes any lingering dirt and grime.

YIELD: 3 cups (about 48 loads)

1 cup baking soda

1 cup washing soda

½ cup citric acid

½ cup salt

20 drops lemon essential oil

¼ cup liquid Castile soap (2 drops per load)

TO MAKE: Combine baking soda, washing soda, citric acid, salt, and lemon essential oil in a covered container. Mix well.

TO USE: Add 1 tablespoon of powdered detergent to your dishwasher's detergent dispenser. Add 2 drops of liquid Castile soap to the compartment as well. Run as usual.

TO STORE: Store indefinitely in covered container in a cool, dark place.

TIP Washing soda, also known as sodium carbonate, is found in the laundry aisle at your grocery or big-box store. Arm & Hammer brand is usually readily available.

LEMON RINSE AID

Using this simple, all-natural rinse aid is a sure way to get sparkling clean dishes every time! Lemon essential oil mixed with vinegar will leave your dishes spotless.

YIELD: 1 cup

1 cup vinegar

10 drops lemon essential oil

TO MAKE: Combine vinegar and lemon essential oil in a squeeze bottle. Shake well.

TO USE: Fill your dishwasher's rinse-aid compartment with mixture.

TO STORE: Store indefinitely in squeeze bottle under sink.

PEPPERMINT ORANGE FOAMING HAND SOAP

Making your own foaming hand soap is easy and will save you money. Orange and peppermint essential oils will cleanse and purify, leaving your hands moisturized and smelling great!

YIELD: 1 cup

2 tablespoons liquid Castile soap

½ teaspoon fractionated coconut oil

½ teaspoon pure aloe vera gel

5 drops orange essential oil

5 drops peppermint essential oil

1 cup distilled water

TO MAKE: Combine all ingredients in a foaming hand soap bottle. Shake well.

TO USE: Add 1–2 pumps of soap to hands and wash well with water.

TO STORE: Store indefinitely in foaming hand soap bottle on counter.

REFRIGERATOR AND FREEZER ODOR REMOVER

Removing odors from your refrigerator and freezer is budget-friendly and easy with this remedy using lemon essential oil! Combining lemon essential oil and baking soda is a great idea due to their odor-removing properties.

YIELD: 1 cup

1 cup baking soda

10 drops lemon essential oil

TO MAKE: Add baking soda to a small bowl or cup. Add lemon essential oil and stir.

TO USE: Place mixture in a bowl or small Mason jar, uncovered, in the back of the refrigerator or freezer.

TO STORE: Keep in refrigerator or freezer and replace every 30 days as needed.

TEA TREE AND EUCALYPTUS CLEANSING SPRAY

Try this purifying spray made with tea tree and eucalyptus essential oils for cleaning surfaces and removing odors in the air. These essential oils, along with vinegar and vodka, make this spray purifying—excellent for all those grimy places in your kitchen!

YIELD: 1½ cups

½ cup vinegar

½ cup vodka

½ cup distilled water

20 drops tea tree essential oil

20 drops eucalyptus essential oil

TO MAKE: Combine all ingredients in a spray bottle. Shake well.

TO USE: Spray on surfaces to be purified. Wipe with a clean paper towel or cloth. To clean the air, spray around the room.

TO STORE: Store indefinitely in spray bottle.

LEMON SINK CLEANER

Removing stains in your sink is easy with this all-natural scrub. Using lemon essential oil is the key to brightening your sink to a shine!

YIELD: 1 application of Lemon Sink Cleaner

½ cup baking soda

10 drops lemon essential oil

½ lemon

TO MAKE: Combine baking soda and lemon essential oil in a small bowl. Mix well.

TO USE: Sprinkle baking-soda mixture into sink. Using the ½ lemon, scrub the baking-soda mixture in the sink. Allow to sit for 10 minutes and scrub again. Rinse well with water.

LAVENDER AND LEMON KITCHEN WIPES

Store-bought kitchen cleansing wipes can be expensive and full of chemicals. Instead, use this DIY recipe with lavender and lemon essential oils, which both purify and leave a light, clean scent!

YIELD: 1 roll of wipes

1 roll high-quality paper towels

1 cup distilled water

1 cup vinegar

2 tablespoons liquid Castile soap

10 drops lavender essential oil

10 drops lemon essential oil

TO MAKE: Lay the paper towel roll horizontally on the table in front of you, then use a serrated knife to cut the roll in half. Use one half of roll now and keep one half of roll for next use. Next, in a covered container or jar large enough to accommodate the cut paper towel roll, combine water, vinegar, soap, and essential oils. Mix well. Place paper towel roll half in the container and cover. The paper towels will soak up the mixture over the course of several hours. Remove the cardboard tube from the paper towel roll and discard. Cover container until needed.

TO USE: Pull from the center of the roll and use paper towels to wipe surfaces clean.

TO STORE: Store indefinitely in covered container.

KITCHEN POT AND PAN SCRUBBER

Scrubbing your pots and pans doesn't have to be a chore with this easy pot and pan scrubber. Made with orange, lemon, or lime essential oil, it will cut through grease with ease!

YIELD: 1 application of Kitchen Pot and Pan Scrubber

½ cup baking soda

4 drops citrus essential oils (orange, lemon, or lime, or a combination)

Vinegar, as needed

TO MAKE: Combine baking soda and essential oils in a shaker jar. Mix well.

TO USE: Sprinkle the baking-soda mixture over the bottoms of your pots and pans. Pour in enough vinegar to cover the bottom of each. Let sit for several minutes. Scrub with a soft scrub brush and allow to sit longer if needed. Rinse with hot water.

TO STORE: Store baking-soda mixture indefinitely in shaker jar under sink.

HOMEMADE KITCHEN DEGREASER

Clean your entire kitchen and get rid of grease and grime with this homemade orange essential oil degreaser and cleaner. Orange essential oil cuts through the grease with ease and leaves a fresh, clean scent!

YIELD: 1 gallon, or 1 application of Homemade Kitchen Degreaser

½ gallon hot water

½ gallon vinegar

½ cup baking soda

20-30 drops orange essential oil

TO MAKE: Combine water, vinegar, and baking soda in a large bucket. Mix in orange essential oil.

TO USE: Using a clean kitchen cloth or sponge dipped in degreaser, wipe down kitchen from top to bottom, paying special attention to the stove hood and cabinets. You can also add this to a spray bottle and refill the bottle as needed.

BUTCHER BLOCK AND WOODEN CUTTING BOARD CLEANER

You may know that it's best to avoid soaking your wooden butcher blocks and cutting boards in water to clean them. Using this easy, all-natural method packed with lemon essential oil instead will get them clean and purified without damaging the wood.

YIELD: 1 cup, or 1 application of Butcher Block and Wooden Cutting Board Cleaner

1 cup salt

10 drops lemon essential oil

½ lemon

½ cup vinegar

TO MAKE: Combine salt and lemon essential oil in a bowl. Mix well.

TO USE: Sprinkle salt mixture onto butcher block or cutting board. Use the ½ lemon to scrub the salt mixture into the board. Allow to sit for several minutes, then pour the vinegar over the salt mixture. Scrub again with the ½ lemon and rinse clean with water.

PEPPERMINT ORANGE REFRIGERATOR DEODORIZING DISKS

Get rid of stinky smells with these Peppermint Orange Refrigerator Deodorizing Disks! Peppermint and orange are the perfect essential oils to remove odors and leave a clean scent.

YIELD: 16 (1-ounce) disks

2 cups baking soda

½ cup distilled water

10 drops orange essential oil

5 drops peppermint essential oil

1-ounce silicone molds or ice cube trays

TO MAKE: Combine baking soda and water in a large bowl. Add in the essential oils. Mix well. Pour the mixture into the molds and allow to sit uncovered until it hardens. Hardening could take one night or several days, depending on the humidity in your area.

TO USE: Place 1 deodorizing disk at the back of your refrigerator. Replace as the scent fades.

TO STORE: Store unused disks indefinitely in a covered container or jar in a cool, dark place.

KITCHEN SPONGE PURIFIER

Sponges can be a breeding ground for bacteria and can become stinky fast. Freshen up with this simple recipe that uses lemon essential oil and your microwave!

YIELD: 1 cup, or 1 application of Kitchen Sponge Purifier

1 cup water

2 drops lemon essential oil

TO MAKE: Combine water and lemon essential oil in a bowl. Mix well.

TO USE: Soak your sponge in the mixture. Squeeze out excess water and place sponge in the microwave. Microwave on high for 60 seconds. Repeat every few days to keep your sponges fresh and odor-free!

FOOD ODOR ELIMINATOR

Cooking can leave behind odors that you don't want in your home—especially when you're expecting company. Freshen up your kitchen with this simple recipe using your favorite essential oils.

YIELD: 1 application of Food Odor Eliminator

Small saucepan filled ¾ of the way full with water

10 drops essential oil of your choice (lemon, lime, orange, clove, lemongrass, cinnamon, and peppermint are great choices)

TO MAKE: Place saucepan of water on stove. Add essential oil to the water.

TO USE: Turn heat to low and bring to a simmer to remove cooking odors and freshen the air.

TRASHCAN DEODORIZER DISKS

Everyone knows that trashcans are smelly. Keep that smell where it belongs with these pleasant trashcan deodorizing disks that use the cleansing, kitchen-friendly smell of pine essential oil.

YIELD: 8 (1-ounce) disks

1 cup baking soda

¼ cup distilled water

10 drops pine essential oil

1-ounce silicone molds or ice cube trays

TO MAKE: Combine baking soda, water, and essential oil in a bowl. Mix well. Pour into mold and allow to sit uncovered to harden for 24 hours or more.

TO USE: Place 1 deodorizing disk in the bottom of the trashcan. Replace every 30 days.

TO STORE: Store indefinitely in a covered container or jar in a cool, dark place.

TARNISH REMOVER

Remove tarnish easily with the help of lemon essential oil and without chemicals! This Tarnish Remover is easy and guaranteed to remove any discoloration on your silver.

YIELD: 3 cups, or 1 application of Tarnish Remover

1 (13" × 9") aluminum pan

½ cup baking soda

3 cups boiling water

5 drops lemon essential oil

TO MAKE: Place silver in the bottom of the aluminum pan. (Note: This pan must be aluminum for this recipe to work as promised.) Sprinkle baking soda over silver. Add water and lemon essential oil to the pan, covering the silver.

TO USE: Allow the silver to sit while the tarnish disappears. Depending how badly the silver is tarnished, this may take 1–10 minutes. When it's gone, remove the silver from the pan, wipe clean with a soft cloth, rinse, and dry with a lint-free cloth.

SILVER CLEANER POLISH

Cleaning your silver is easy with this all-natural polish recipe. The lemon essential oil helps your silver get extra clean and sparkling!

YIELD: ¼ cup, or 1 application of Silver Cleaner Polish

½ cup baking soda

¼ cup hot water

10 drops lemon essential oil

TO MAKE: Combine baking soda, hot water, and lemon essential oil in a bowl. Mix well to make a paste.

TO USE: Using a cloth or a toothbrush, apply the paste to silver and scrub well. Rinse with water and buff dry.

PRODUCE CLEANER

Organic produce is best, but it's not always available, leaving you with produce covered in chemicals and grime. Fortunately, the cleansing properties of lemon essential oil are perfect to make sure your produce is clean and ready to eat, no matter where it came from.

YIELD: 2 cups, or 1 application of Produce Cleaner

2 cups vinegar

10 drops lemon essential oil

TO MAKE: Combine vinegar and lemon essential oil in a large bowl. Mix well.

TO USE: Add uncut fruits and vegetables to bowl and let soak for 5–10 minutes. Drain produce and rinse with clean water. Dry with paper towels before eating or storing.

BURN SOOTHER

Take the sting out of accidental kitchen burns using lavender essential oil. Lavender is known to cleanse and soothe, which makes it perfect for burns.

YIELD: 1 application of Burn Soother

Lavender essential oil, as needed

TO USE: For minor burns from hot pans in the kitchen, apply several drops of lavender essential oil directly on burn. Reapply every 15–20 minutes as needed.

TIP Do not apply to broken or cut skin. Also, note that this Burn Soother is meant to be used to treat minor burns. For more serious burns, call 911 or consult a doctor.

PEPPERMINT-FLAVORED TOOTHPICKS

Peppermint essential oil has long been used for its odor-destroying properties, so it's perfect for this recipe! Freshen breath with this powerful essential oil with these flavored toothpicks that you can make at home naturally!

YIELD: ½ box of toothpicks

½ box wooden toothpicks

Small jar with lid

10 drops peppermint essential oil

TO MAKE: Add toothpicks to the bottom of your jar. Pour essential oil drops over the toothpicks. Cover with lid and shake well. Allow toothpicks to sit overnight to allow the essential oil to soak in.

TO USE: Use toothpicks as normal.

TO STORE: Store indefinitely in covered jar. Refresh with a drop or two of peppermint oil as needed.

PLASTIC FOOD STORAGE CONTAINER CLEANER

Plastic food storage containers are perfect for storing your leftover food but can get stinky and develop stains over time. This all-natural cleaner uses lemon essential oil to get them as good as new!

YIELD: ½ cup, or 1 application of Plastic Food Storage Container Cleaner

½ cup vinegar

5 drops lemon essential oil

¼ cup baking soda

TO MAKE: Combine vinegar and essential oil in a small glass or bowl. Mix well.

TO USE: Sprinkle baking soda into the bottom of your container. Pour in vinegar-oil mixture. Scrub with a soft brush, then allow to sit for 10–20 minutes. Scrub again and rinse clean.

TIP   Depending on how large your container is, you may be able to clean several containers with this recipe.

CHAPTER 5

Bathroom

One of my favorite places to use nontoxic solutions is in the bathroom. Peppermint, orange, lemon, and lavender essential oils all have cleansing properties and smell amazing, and pine, eucalyptus, and tea tree essential oils will purify as well as any commercial product you can buy—and they are safe for the entire family! So, while bathrooms aren't usually high on everyone's list of favorite places to clean, you'll enjoy using products ranging from Lavender and Lemon Bathroom Surface Cleaner to No-Scrub Toilet Bowl Cleaner to get your bathroom squeaky clean and sparkling. Refresh and renew your spirit with the calming fragrance of lavender and orange essential oils in bathroom sprays, cleansing wipes, and scrubs. You'll also find some personal care solutions that you're going to love, like the foaming bath bombs that you can enjoy when you're ready to relax at the end of the day. Get the kids involved and keep your bathroom in green, clean condition the all-natural way!

RUST REMOVER

Whether your rust issues are big or small, this recipe is sure to take care of them without the harsh chemicals. Lemon essential oil will cut through rust in no time.

YIELD: 1 cup, or 1 application of Rust Remover

1 cup borax

½ cup vinegar

20 drops lemon essential oil

TO MAKE: Combine borax and vinegar in a bowl. Mix well to make a paste. Stir in lemon essential oil.

TO USE: Apply paste to rust. Allow to sit for 30 minutes. Scrub well with a brush to remove rust. Rinse well. Repeat if needed.

LIME STAIN REMOVER

Having hard water can produce lime stains that are hard to get rid of with conventional cleaners. Try this DIY method with lime essential oil to get rid of stains fast!

YIELD: 2 cups, or 1 application of Lime Stain Remover

1 cup vinegar

1 cup liquid Castile soap

20 drops lime essential oil

TO MAKE: Combine all ingredients in a spray bottle or large bowl. Mix well.

TO USE: Apply solution to lime stains with a soft cloth, then allow to sit for 10 minutes. Scrub well with a brush or cloth. Rinse. Repeat if needed.

MOLD AND MILDEW REMOVER

Mold and mildew can seem scary, but when you know how to attack the problem head on with a natural, chemical-free cleaner, you'll have it cleared up in no time! This product uses tea tree essential oil, a natural cleanser, to remove mold and mildew fast.

YIELD: 1 cup

1 cup vinegar

20 drops tea tree essential oil

TO MAKE: Combine vinegar and tea tree essential oil in a spray bottle. Shake well.

TO USE: Saturate mold or mildew with solution. Allow to soak for 5 minutes. Scrub clean.

TO STORE: Store indefinitely in spray bottle.

EUCALYPTUS TOILET CLEANER

Try this toilet cleaner that is not only easy to make but is also packed with the purifying properties of eucalyptus essential oil, which will freshen your toilet bowl while cutting through grime!

YIELD: ½ cup, or 1 application of Eucalyptus Toilet Cleaner

½ cup baking soda

½ cup vinegar

10 drops eucalyptus essential oil

TO MAKE: Add all ingredients to toilet bowl.

TO USE: Using a scrub brush, clean the inside of the toilet thoroughly. Allow to sit for several minutes, then flush.

SANITIZING TOILET SPRAY

Apply this Sanitizing Toilet Spray to the entire toilet and bowl and watch as the tea tree and peppermint essential oils purify and remove odors with ease.

YIELD: 2¼ cups

1 cup distilled water

1 cup vinegar

¼ cup liquid Castile soap

10 drops tea tree essential oil

10 drops peppermint essential oil

TO MAKE: Combine all ingredients in a large spray bottle. Shake well.

TO USE: Spray on toilet surfaces and wipe with a clean cloth. Spray inside bowl and use a brush to scrub well.

TO STORE: Store indefinitely in spray bottle.

NO-SCRUB TOILET BOWL CLEANER

For those stubborn rings around the toilet, use this no-scrub solution with pine and eucalyptus essential oils to get it clean the easy way!

YIELD: 1 application of No-Scrub Toilet Bowl Cleaner

1 cup borax

1 cup vinegar

2 cups water

10 drops pine essential oil

10 drops eucalyptus essential oil

TO MAKE: Combine all ingredients in a large bucket. Mix well.

TO USE: Pour solution into toilet and allow to sit overnight. In the morning, flush to reveal a clean bowl!

LAVENDER AND LEMON BATHROOM SURFACE CLEANER

This cleaner is perfect for all bathroom surfaces, including mirrors and fixtures. The lemon and lavender essential oils will purify and add shine at the same time!

YIELD: 2¼ cups

1 cup vinegar

1 cup distilled water

¼ cup rubbing alcohol

10 drops lemon essential oil

10 drops lavender essential oil

TO MAKE: Combine all ingredients in a large spray bottle. Shake well.

TO USE: Spray on bathroom surfaces and wipe clean with a lint-free cloth.

TO STORE: Store indefinitely in spray bottle.

TIP   I like to keep one bottle in the upstairs linen closet and one in the downstairs closet, one for each bathroom. I then easily wipe down the bathroom surfaces at the end of the day, keeping them smelling fresh and clean.

TEA TREE AND EUCALYPTUS BATHROOM PURIFIER

Tea tree and eucalyptus essential oils are workhorses against dirt and grime. Combining them in this bathroom purifier guarantees the cleanest and freshest-smelling surfaces possible!

YIELD: 1 cup

½ cup vinegar

½ cup vodka

10 drops tea tree essential oil

10 drops eucalyptus essential oil

TO MAKE: Combine all ingredients in a spray bottle. Shake well.

TO USE: Apply to surfaces to be cleansed. This can be sprayed on, left for several minutes, then wiped off, or it can be sprayed in the air.

TO STORE: Store indefinitely in spray bottle.

SOAP SCUM REMOVER

Removing soap scum in the bathroom doesn't require much elbow grease when you use this Soap Scum Remover with tea tree essential oil and washing soda. Tea tree essential oil cuts through soap scum and purifies at the same time, making it perfect for this bathroom cleaner.

YIELD: 1 application of Soap Scum Remover

½ cup washing soda

10 drops tea tree essential oil

1 gallon hot water

TO MAKE: Add washing soda and tea tree essential oil to bucket of hot water. Mix well.

TO USE: Wearing gloves to protect your hands from the hot water, dip a sponge into the cleaning solution and wipe down areas containing soap scum. Allow to sit for several minutes, then wipe clean with a clean sponge. Rinse well with water.

ROSEMARY AND LEMON SURFACE SCRUB

Rosemary and lemon essential oils are known to cut through grime, purify, and whiten naturally. Using a recipe with these essential oils is the perfect way to clean without harmful chemicals.

YIELD: 1½ cups, or 1 application of Rosemary and Lemon Surface Scrub

1 cup baking soda

½ cup liquid Castile soap

10 drops rosemary essential oil

10 drops lemon essential oil

TO MAKE: Combine all ingredients in a small bowl. Mix well.

TO USE: Use a sponge to apply mixture and scrub tub and tile clean. Rinse well.

TEA TREE BATHROOM SURFACE SCRUB

This is a great multipurpose cleaner that is easy on your surfaces yet strong enough to brighten and purify. Use this chemical-free cleanser to keep your bathroom spotless!

YIELD: 1 cup, or 1 application of Tea Tree Bathroom Surface Scrub

¾ cup baking soda

¼ cup liquid Castile soap

1 teaspoon hydrogen peroxide

10 drops tea tree essential oil

TO MAKE: Combine all ingredients in a small bowl. Mix well.

TO USE: Wet surface to be cleaned and apply mixture with a sponge. Allow to sit for several minutes, then scrub clean. Rinse well.

BATHROOM GROUT CLEANER

To get your grout looking new again, use this simple grout cleaner with tea tree essential oil. Tea tree essential oil both cleans and prevents mold and mildew from forming, which is perfect for use in the bathroom. Use this cleaner often to keep grout looking its best!

YIELD: 2 cups, or 1 application of Bathroom Grout Cleaner

2 cups baking soda

½ cup warm water

10 drops tea tree essential oil

TO MAKE: Combine baking soda and water in a bowl. Mix well to make a paste. Add tea tree essential oil and mix well.

TO USE: Apply to grout lines using a sponge, a small brush, or an old toothbrush. Scrub well, then allow to sit for several minutes. Scrub again and rinse with clean water.

LEMON-SCENTED BATHROOM GLASS CLEANER

Why pay for store-bought glass cleaner when you can make your own at home for next to nothing? The lemon essential oil in this recipe keeps your glass sparkling clean.

YIELD: 2½ cups

1 cup distilled water

1 cup vinegar

¼ cup rubbing alcohol

¼ teaspoon liquid Castile soap

10 drops lemon essential oil

TO MAKE: Combine all ingredients in a large spray bottle. Shake well.

TO USE: Spray on windows and glass. Wipe clean with a lint-free cloth or paper towels.

TO STORE: Store indefinitely in spray bottle.

TIP Using newspaper is a great way to get windows clean and lint-free! Some theorize that since newspaper is specifically made to hold the ink, it also grabs any dirt that's on your windows, mirrors, or other glass surfaces and holds it tight—safely and inexpensively cleaning these hard-to-clean surfaces.

TOILET PAPER ROLL AIR FRESHENER

Want to freshen your bathroom every time you use your toilet paper roll? This toilet roll air freshener with lavender and lemon essential oils will keep your room smelling fresh and clean with each pull of the roll!

YIELD: 1 toilet paper roll

2 drops lavender essential oil

2 drops lemon essential oil

TO MAKE: Add lavender and lemon essential oils to the inside of the cardboard center of your toilet paper roll.

TO USE: Use toilet paper as normal. Every time you pull the paper, the roll will release the smells and benefits of the essential oils that have been added inside.

TOOTHBRUSH HOLDER CLEANER

You may not think about it, but your toothbrush holder is one place that gets dirty and grimy in a hurry. Clean it up with this easy solution that uses tea tree essential oil to purify and cleanse fast!

YIELD: 2 cups, or 1 application of Toothbrush Holder Cleaner

1 cup vinegar

1 cup hot water

10 drops tea tree essential oil

TO MAKE: Combine all ingredients in a large bowl. Mix well.

TO USE: Place toothbrush holder in vinegar solution. Allow to sit for several minutes. Using an old toothbrush, scrub the holder clean, paying extra attention to all the little spaces that are hard to reach. Rinse clean with hot water.

TOOTHBRUSH CLEANER

Keep your toothbrush clean and free of yuck with this all-natural Toothbrush Cleaner. Tea tree essential oil is great for purifying, and is a wonderful choice for this cleaner.

YIELD: ½ cup, or 1 application of Toothbrush Cleaner

½ cup vinegar

2-3 drops tea tree essential oil

TO MAKE: Combine vinegar and tea tree essential oil in a small glass. Mix well.

TO USE: Add toothbrush to glass bristle-side down and allow to sit for at least 10 minutes. Rinse well with hot water before use.

TEA TREE COMB AND HAIRBRUSH CLEANER

Clean your combs and brushes once a month to remove dirt and oily residue from natural oils and hair products. Using tea tree essential oil will help purify and get your comb and brush squeaky clean without chemicals.

YIELD: ½ cup, or 1 application of Tea Tree Comb and Hairbrush Cleaner

Enough hot water to fill your sink

½ cup vinegar

2 tablespoons liquid Castile soap

5 drops tea tree essential oil

TO MAKE: Fill your bathroom sink or a clean bucket with hot water. Add in vinegar, soap, and tea tree essential oil.

TO USE: Remove all hair from your combs and brushes, then place combs and brushes in the cleaning solution. Allow to sit for 10–15 minutes. Using your hands or a small scrub brush, scrub clean. Rinse thoroughly with clean water and allow to air-dry before putting back in your drawer.

LAVENDER FOAMING HAND SOAP

Lavender essential oil is a wonderful addition to this basic foaming hand soap recipe. It leaves your hands clean and smells great! Making this hand soap yourself will save lots of money in the long run.

YIELD: 1 cup

½ cup liquid Castile soap

1 teaspoon fractionated coconut oil or almond oil

1 teaspoon vegetable glycerin

10 drops lavender essential oil

½ cup distilled water

TO MAKE: Combine Castile soap, coconut oil, glycerin, and lavender essential oil in a foaming hand soap container. Next add water. Replace lid and shake gently.

TO USE: Add 1–2 pumps of soap to hands and wash well with water.

TO STORE: Store indefinitely in foaming hand soap container on sink.

FOAMING DRAIN CLEANER

Drains can get stinky and yucky from time to time. Use this Foaming Drain Cleaner that has the cleansing powers of baking soda, vinegar, and lemon essential oil to break up dirt and leave a fresh smell.

YIELD: 1 cup, or 1 application of Foaming Drain Cleaner

1 cup baking soda

10 drops lemon essential oil

1 cup vinegar

TO MAKE: Combine baking soda and lemon essential oil in a bowl. Mix well.

TO USE: Pour baking-soda mixture down the drain, followed by vinegar. Allow to sit for several minutes, then flush well with hot water.

ORANGE TOILET BOMBS

Drop these fizzing toilet bombs into your toilet to naturally scrub it clean. Orange essential oil is known for its cleansing and odor-removing properties, and it leaves a fresh, clean scent as well!

YIELD: Approximately 16 bombs

1 cup baking soda

¼ cup citric acid

1 teaspoon vinegar

20 drops orange essential oil

1-ounce silicone molds or ice cube trays

TO MAKE: Combine the baking soda and citric acid in a bowl. Mix well. Then, *slowly* add the vinegar to the baking-soda mixture, using a fork to slowly stir together. Next, carefully add the orange essential oil. Add the paste to the molds and allow to dry out and harden completely, uncovered for a few hours to overnight, before removing.

TO USE: Add toilet bomb to a clean toilet bowl, allow to dissolve, and flush.

TO STORE: Store indefinitely in a covered jar in a cool, dark place.

DAILY SHOWER CLEANER

Keep your shower sparkling clean with this Daily Shower Cleaner containing orange and peppermint essential oils. The essential oils cut through dirt, grime, and soap scum while purifying at the same time.

YIELD: ½ cup

¼ cup vinegar

¼ cup liquid Castile soap

5 drops orange essential oil

5 drops peppermint essential oil

TO MAKE: Add vinegar, soap, and essential oils to a dish wand with a scrubbing sponge on the end.

TO USE: After your shower, scrub down the shower with the wand. Rinse completely with warm water.

TO STORE: Store indefinitely in dish wand.

HARD WATER STAIN REMOVER

Tough-to-remove hard water stains in the bathroom are no match for this DIY cleanser. The tea tree essential oil used in this mixture cuts right through the stains and purifies at the same time.

YIELD: 1 cup

1 cup vinegar

20 drops tea tree essential oil

TO MAKE: Combine vinegar and tea tree essential oil in a spray bottle. Mix well.

TO USE: Spray on hard water stains. Allow to sit for several minutes, then scrub with a brush. Rinse clean. Repeat as needed.

TO STORE: Store indefinitely in spray bottle.

SHOWER HEAD CLEANER

Removing hard water stains from your shower head to help water flow freely is easy with this simple recipe containing lemon essential oil.

YIELD: 1 application of Shower Head Cleaner

1 cup vinegar

10 drops lemon essential oil

1 gallon- or quart-sized zip-top plastic bag, depending on the size of your showerhead

1 rubber band

TO MAKE: Combine vinegar and lemon essential oil in the zip-top bag.

TO USE: Place plastic bag over shower head, making sure the mixture is covering the shower head. Use the rubber band to secure bag around the neck of the shower head to keep it in place. Allow to sit for 10 minutes. Remove bag, then use a small brush to scrub the shower head clean. Rinse well with warm water.

LAVENDER AND TEA TREE CLEANSING WIPES

These cleansing wipes are good to use on your face and hands, and even as diaper-changing wipes for your small children. Lavender and tea tree essential oils are both purifying and wonderful for soothing skin. Leave these wipes in your bathroom or take them with you on the go.

YIELD: 1 roll of wipes

1 roll high-quality paper towels

2 cups distilled water

1 tablespoon liquid Castile soap

1 tablespoon fractionated coconut oil

10 drops lavender essential oil

5 drops tea tree essential oil

TO MAKE: Lay the paper towel roll horizontally on the table in front of you, then use a serrated knife to cut the roll in half. Use one half of roll now and keep one half of roll for next use. Add water, soap, coconut oil, and essential oils to a bowl. Mix well. Remove the cardboard tube from the paper towel roll and discard. Place paper towel roll half in a plastic container large enough to accommodate it (such as an empty baby wipes container). Pour the water mixture over the paper towels and allow to sit for an hour to absorb the liquid.

TO USE: Pull wipes from the center of the roll and use to clean hands or wash face, or to keep in your bathroom as personal cleansing wipes.

TO STORE: Store in container for up to 2 weeks.

VARIATION Instead of paper towels, buy cloth wipes, cut up an old T-shirt, or use washcloths.

STRESS-FREE BATH BOMBS

Drop one of these in your bath and relax! Lavender essential oil is known to calm and renew your mind and body. It's a great way to end the day!

YIELD: Approximately 80 (1-ounce) bombs

1¾ cups baking soda

1 cup citric acid

2 cups cornstarch

1 tablespoon fractionated coconut oil or almond oil

Distilled water, as needed

10 drops lavender essential oil

1-ounce silicone molds or ice cube trays

TO MAKE: Sift baking soda, citric acid, and cornstarch through a sieve into a bowl to remove larger chunks, or use a fork to mash into a fine powder. Add in coconut or almond oil and mix well with a fork. Fill a small spray bottle with distilled water and lightly spritz the baking-soda mixture. Mix well until the mixture becomes the consistency of sand that can be molded with your hands. Add lavender essential oil and mix well. Add the mixture to the molds and allow to harden uncovered for 3 hours before removing.

TO USE: Pop 1 bath bomb into your bath water and enjoy!

TO STORE: Store indefinitely in a covered container or jar in a cool, dark place.

VARIATION

Before adding essential oil, divide mixture among several bowls and add in different essential oils to make other scents. You can also add a couple of drops of food coloring to your water bottle to make colorful bath bombs!

LINEN CLOSET SPRAY

Leave a lasting scent in your linen closet by using this spray. The lavender essential oil freshens the all-natural way!

YIELD: ¼ cup

¼ cup distilled water

10 drops lavender essential oil

TO MAKE: Combine water and lavender essential oil in a small spray bottle. Shake well.

TO USE: From time to time, spritz towels with lavender spray.

TO STORE: Store indefinitely in spray bottle on shelf in linen closet.

SCENTED BATH TOWEL SHEETS

Scent your bath towels and keep them fresh by putting these easy DIY scented sheets between your folded and stored towels. Lemongrass essential oil removes odors and provides an uplifting scent!

YIELD: 4 sheets

1 paper towel

4 drops lemongrass essential oil

TO MAKE: The number of towels you have to keep fresh will determine how many paper towels you'll need for this recipe. Take one paper towel and cut it into fourths. Add 1 drop of lemongrass essential oil to each sheet. Repeat for however many towels you have.

TO USE: Place scented sheets in between bath towels.

TO STORE: Store indefinitely in the linen closet.

SHOWER CURTAIN SOAP SCUM REMOVER

Soap scum is bound to find its way to your shower curtain. Fortunately, this recipe using tea tree essential oil can remove it easily and keep things clean longer!

YIELD: ¼ cup, or 1 application of Shower Curtain Soap Scum Remover

¼ cup vinegar

10 drops tea tree essential oil

TO MAKE: Combine vinegar and tea tree essential oil in a measuring cup. Mix well.

TO USE: Remove shower curtain from shower rod and place in your washing machine. Add vinegar mixture to your rinse-cycle container. If you don't have a rinse-cycle container, add to your final rinse-cycle water. Wash your shower curtain as normal with your favorite detergent, such as Large-Batch Powdered Laundry Soap (see recipe in Chapter 6). Remove from washer when done and hang to dry.

JEWELRY CLEANER

Use this gentle, all-natural recipe to make your jewelry sparkling clean the nontoxic way. Lemon essential oil cuts through dirt and grime and leaves your jewelry shining every time!

YIELD: 1 cup, or 1 application of Jewelry Cleaner

1 cup hot water

1 teaspoon baking soda

5 drops lemon essential oil

TO MAKE: Combine water, baking soda, and lemon essential oil in a bowl. Mix well.

TO USE: Add jewelry to the water mixture. Allow to sit for several minutes. Scrub lightly with a small brush or old toothbrush. Rinse well. Dry with a lint-free cloth. Discard mixture.

TIP   Don't use this recipe on jewelry that is delicate, such as pearls. It's made for metals such as silver and gold.

MAKEUP BRUSH CLEANER

Using makeup brushes daily can leave them caked with a mixture of makeup and dirt. Use this DIY Makeup Brush Cleaner once a week to keep them looking like new. Tea tree and lemon essential oils cleanse and purify, keeping your brushes clean longer.

YIELD: 1 cup, or 1 application of Makeup Brush Cleaner

1 cup hot water

2 tablespoons vinegar

¼ teaspoon liquid Castile soap

5 drops tea tree essential oil

5 drops lemon essential oil

TO MAKE: Combine water, vinegar, soap, and tea tree and lemon essential oils in a large cup. Mix well.

TO USE: Dip makeup brush into the solution and swirl around, pressing against the bottom to "scrub" lightly. Rinse brush well with cold water until the water runs clean. Using a paper towel, gently squeeze out water and reshape brush. Lay flat on paper towels to dry.

ALCOHOL-FREE FLEXIBLE-HOLD HAIRSPRAY

Store-bought hairsprays are full of chemicals and unfamiliar ingredients, but you can make this healthier and cheaper hairspray at home! The rosemary essential oil adds a pleasant scent while stimulating your hair follicles, thus strengthening your hair.

YIELD: 1 cup

1 cup distilled water

2 tablespoons white sugar

10 drops rosemary essential oil

TO MAKE: Boil water. Stir in sugar to dissolve. Remove from heat and allow to cool to room temperature. Add in rosemary essential oil and transfer mixture to a spray bottle with a fine-mist spray top.

TO USE: Spray hair as normal.

TO STORE: Store indefinitely in spray bottle.

CITRUS LAVENDER FLEXIBLE-HOLD HAIRSPRAY

Leave a clean, fresh scent in your hair while providing flexible hold with this all-natural hair spray. The orange and lavender essential oils will remove odors, provide a pleasant scent, and protect your hair from damage. This is sure to become one of your favorite hair care products!

YIELD: 1 cup

1 cup distilled water

2 tablespoons white sugar

1 tablespoon vodka

5 drops orange essential oil

5 drops lavender essential oil

TO MAKE: Boil water. Stir in sugar to dissolve. Remove from heat and allow to cool to room temperature. Add in vodka and essential oils. Transfer mixture to a spray bottle with a fine-mist spray top.

TO USE: Spray hair as normal.

TO STORE: Store indefinitely in spray bottle.

DETANGLER SPRAY

Make your own Detangler Spray at home instead of overpaying at the store! Rosemary and lavender essential oils will leave your hair smelling fresh and will keep it knot-free and looking great.

YIELD: ½ cup

½ cup distilled water

1 tablespoon conditioner

5 drops lavender essential oil

5 drops rosemary essential oil

TO MAKE: Combine all ingredients in a spray bottle with a fine-mist spray top. Shake well.

TO USE: Spray lightly on hair and brush out tangles as needed.

TO STORE: Store indefinitely in spray bottle.

DRY SHAMPOO FOR LIGHT HAIR

Busy? Try this dry shampoo recipe with rosemary and tea tree essential oils to remove odors while soaking up excess oils. It's the perfect fix for busy days when you don't have time to hop in the shower, or for when you want to freshen up after a workout.

YIELD: ½ cup

½ cup arrowroot powder

2 drops rosemary essential oil

2 drops tea tree essential oil

TO MAKE: Combine all ingredients in a bowl. Mix well. Transfer mixture to a small covered jar.

TO USE: Dip a makeup brush into the powder mixture. Tap off excess powder on edge of jar. Apply to roots of hair and slightly down strands of hair as well. Using a hair brush, brush your hair from root to tip to work in the dry shampoo. Allow to sit for several minutes, then style as usual.

TO STORE: Store indefinitely in covered jar.

DRY SHAMPOO FOR DARK HAIR

If you have dark hair, this recipe is for you! With the addition of cocoa powder to darken up the arrowroot powder, this dry shampoo will blend right in with your hair.

YIELD: ½ cup

¼ cup arrowroot powder

2 drops rosemary essential oil

2 drops tea tree essential oil

¼ cup unsweetened cocoa powder

TO MAKE: Combine arrowroot powder and essential oils in a bowl. Add cocoa powder, mixing well. Transfer mixture to a small covered jar.

TO USE: Dip a makeup brush into the powder mixture. Tap off excess powder on edge of jar. Apply to roots of hair and slightly down strands of hair as well. Using a hair brush, brush hair from root to tip to work in the dry shampoo. Allow to sit for several minutes, then style as usual.

TO STORE: Store indefinitely in covered jar.

SHOWER VAPORIZERS

Stuffy nose and head? These Shower Vaporizers will have you cleared right up! Lavender, lemon, and peppermint essential oils are the perfect combination to tackle unpleasant symptoms from colds and allergies.

YIELD: 20–24 (1-ounce) disks

1 cup baking soda

½ cup cornstarch

¼ cup distilled water

10 drops lavender essential oil

10 drops lemon essential oil

10 drops peppermint essential oil

1-ounce silicone molds or ice cube trays

TO MAKE: Combine baking soda and cornstarch in a bowl. Add in water and mix to make a paste. If needed, add a couple more tablespoons of water for a paste-like consistency. Mix in essential oils. Transfer mixture to molds and allow to sit uncovered for several hours to overnight to harden.

TO USE: Place 1 vaporizing disk in the bottom of the shower where the water will run over it. Each disk will last through one shower.

TO STORE: Store indefinitely in a covered container or jar in a cool, dark place.

SUN RELIEF SPRAY

Too much sun? Try this all-natural Sun Relief Spray that uses lavender essential oil to soothe, peppermint essential oil to cool, and frankincense essential oil to help skin feel refreshed fast!

YIELD: ¾ cup

½ cup distilled water

2 tablespoons pure aloe vera gel

20 drops lavender essential oil

10 drops peppermint essential oil

10 drops frankincense essential oil

TO MAKE: Combine all ingredients in a bowl. Pour into a spray bottle with a fine-mist spray top. Shake well.

TO USE: Spray on skin every 30 minutes as needed.

TO STORE: Store indefinitely in spray bottle.

ALL-NATURAL BEACH CREAM

Sunscreens can be full of extra chemicals that can be absorbed into your body. Take the all-natural route and use natural ingredients that are packed with SPF protection. Carrot seed and myrrh essential oils are the best options for a natural SPF!

YIELD: 1 cup

½ cup unrefined coconut oil

½ cup shea butter

2 tablespoons zinc oxide powder

20 drops carrot seed essential oil

20 drops myrrh essential oil

TO MAKE: Make a double boiler by simmering 1 cup of water in a pot on the stove. Place a metal bowl slightly smaller than the pot over the water, then add coconut oil to the bowl and stir to melt completely. Remove the bowl from the heat and add in shea butter. Stir until melted. Add zinc oxide powder and mix well with a hand whisk or a mixer. Allow mixture to cool until it starts to harden, approximately 30 minutes to an hour. Once mixture is cool, add essential oils. Using a mixer, whip beach cream for 3–5 minutes until it is creamy and ingredients are completely combined. Place in a covered glass jar.

TO USE: Apply to skin before heading into the sun. Reapply every 30 minutes.

TO STORE: Store for up to 1 month in covered jar in a cool, dark place.

FOOT-SOFTENING SOAK

Refresh tired, dry feet with this easy DIY Foot-Softening Soak. Tea tree essential oil purifies, peppermint essential oil provides a cool sensation, and lavender essential oil soothes your skin. It's a great way to end the day!

YIELD: 1 application of Foot-Softening Soak

Warm water, as needed

1 cup Epsom salts

¼ cup coconut, almond, or olive oil

5 drops tea tree essential oil

5 drops peppermint essential oil

5 drops lavender essential oil

TO MAKE: Fill a large basin, tub, or shallow bucket ⅔ of the way full with warm water. Add Epsom salts and stir to dissolve. Add in coconut, almond, or olive oil along with tea tree, peppermint, and lavender essential oils.

TO USE: Place feet in water mixture and allow to soak until water cools completely. Remove feet from water and dry thoroughly. Follow up with your favorite moisturizer or the Cooling Foot Moisturizer found in this chapter.

COOLING FOOT MOISTURIZER

Take care of hot, tired feet with this all-natural Cooling Foot Moisturizer! Peppermint essential oil provides a cooling sensation along with odor-fighting properties, making this a great treat for your feet at the end of the day.

YIELD: 1 cup

½ cup coconut oil

½ cup shea butter

10 drops peppermint essential oil

TO MAKE: Whip together coconut oil and shea butter with a hand mixer for 3–5 minutes or until light and fluffy. Add in peppermint essential oil and mix well. Transfer mixture to a covered jar.

TO USE: Apply to feet as needed to cool and refresh.

TO STORE: Store for up to 1 month in covered jar.

GRAPEFRUIT AND ORANGE SUGAR SCRUB

Uplift and calm your body and mind with grapefruit and orange essential oils. This sugar scrub is perfect for increasing circulation while exfoliating skin!

YIELD: 1 cup

1 cup white sugar

¼ cup coconut oil, melted

10 drops grapefruit essential oil

10 drops orange essential oil

TO MAKE: Combine sugar and melted coconut oil in a bowl. Add grapefruit and orange essential oils and mix well. Transfer mixture to a covered jar.

TO USE: Wet skin, then apply a small amount of sugar scrub. Massage and scrub skin. Rinse well with water and pat dry.

TO STORE: Store for up to 1 month in covered jar.

TEETH-WHITENING PASTE

Whiten teeth the natural way with this homemade recipe! Lemon essential oil is known to whiten and brighten, and is even more powerful with baking soda. Use this weekly for best results.

YIELD: 1 application of Teeth-Whitening Paste

1 tablespoon baking soda

¼ teaspoon distilled water

5 drops lemon essential oil

TO MAKE: Combine baking soda and water in a small bowl. Mix well to make a paste. Mix in lemon essential oil.

TO USE: Wet toothbrush and place in mixture. Apply paste to teeth and brush gently. Allow to sit for 1 minute, then rinse off completely.

CALMING LAVENDER AND ORANGE SPRAY

Use this all-natural spray on yourself or on your bed linens to relax and unwind, any time of day. Lavender and orange essential oils are known to relax and calm your mind, making them perfect for this recipe.

YIELD: ¼ cup

¼ cup distilled water

10 drops lavender essential oil

10 drops orange essential oil

TO MAKE: Combine water and essential oils in a small spray bottle with a fine-mist spray top.

TO USE: Spritz on body or bed linens. Breathe deeply and relax.

TO STORE: Store indefinitely in spray bottle.

PICK-ME-UP SPRAY

Peppermint and lemon essential oils are known to uplift, energize, and wake up your mind and body. Take this spray with you and use anytime you need an all-natural pick-me-up!

YIELD: ¼ cup

¼ cup distilled water

10 drops peppermint essential oil

10 drops lemon essential oil

TO MAKE: Combine water and essential oils in a small spray bottle with a fine-mist spray top.

TO USE: Spritz on body or in air. Breathe deeply.

TO STORE: Store indefinitely in spray bottle.

SPLINTER EXTRACTOR

Forget digging out a lodged splinter. Use this all-natural remedy that promises pain-free removal with the cleansing and pain-relieving properties of clove essential oil!

YIELD: 1 application of Splinter Extractor

2-4 drops clove essential oil

TO MAKE: Depending on the size of your splinter, apply 2–4 drops of clove essential oil to the site.

TO USE: Allow to sit for 15–20 minutes, then check to see if splinter has worked its way out enough to grab it with tweezers. If not, reapply oil and wait. Do this until the splinter is far enough out to remove it painlessly.

TOOTHACHE RELIEF

Clove essential oil is a wonderful natural pain reliever. Apply to a painful tooth to relieve pain on contact!

YIELD: 1 application of Toothache Relief

1-2 drops clove essential oil

TO USE: Apply 1–2 drops of clove essential oil to tooth and gum area where pain occurs. Reapply every 30 minutes.

NOTE: This recipe is not a substitute for seeing a dentist. If pain persists, see a dentist.

CHAPTER 6

Laundry

Adding your own DIY, all-natural laundry solutions to your routine is one of the best ways to save money and safely remove toxins from your home! With a few staples in your laundry room—liquid Castile soap, baking soda, washing soda, vinegar, and essential oils—you can create nontoxic, eco-friendly solutions that you'll be excited to use again and again. There are several essential oils that are perfect for all your laundry needs—including tea tree, lemon, and orange essential oils, among others—and whether you're adding scent or cleansing and purifying, you'll find a lot of the same oils used again and again. The great thing about these recipes is that you can swap out the essential oils used in some of the recipes for your favorites. Not a fan of lavender in your linen mist? Add lemon essential oil instead. Don't like the smell of pine essential oil? Use tea tree essential oil. It's up to you! In this chapter you'll find recipes for laundry detergents, a fabric softener, and stain removers, as well as general tips to make laundry much more fun. Start making your own laundry soap or fabric softener, and before long, you'll become the laundry expert in your home!

LARGE-BATCH POWDERED LAUNDRY SOAP

This is my favorite laundry soap recipe! This recipe makes such a large amount, you can go months without making more! It also smells great, gets out stains, and brightens your clothes using the combined powers of lavender and lemon essential oils. Mix up a big batch for yourself or share with your friends.

YIELD: 1–2 ounces per load or 243–486 loads

2 bars Fels-Naptha soap

1 (76-ounce) box borax

1 (55-ounce) box washing soda

1 (16-ounce) box baking soda

2 (3-pound) containers OxiClean

50 drops lavender essential oil

50 drops lemon essential oil

TO MAKE: Using a food processor or a hand cheese grater, grate the bars of soap. Then combine all ingredients in a large bucket. Mix well.

TO USE: Save the scoop from the jar of OxiClean and it use to add laundry soap to washing machine. Use 1 scoop for a normal load or 2 scoops for a large load. This recipe is safe for high-efficiency (HE) machines; just place the soap in the drum of the machine before adding clothes.

TO STORE: Store indefinitely in large covered container the soap was mixed in, or a smaller container, on your laundry room shelf. Refill the smaller container from the larger container as needed.

TIP Borax is a naturally occurring mineral that shouldn't be ingested or put in your eyes. There are some debates as to just how safe and "green" this mineral really is. That said, it is commonly used in cleaning recipes. If you're concerned about using borax, do some research to determine if this mineral is right for you or try the borax-free recipe in this chapter.

SMALL-BATCH LAUNDRY SOAP

Want to experiment with different soaps or essential oils? Try whipping up this Small-Batch Laundry Soap. This recipe uses lavender essential oil for a light, clean scent, but you should feel free to add your favorite essential oil for a unique, all-natural washing experience.

YIELD: 8 cups

1 bar Fels-Naptha soap

2 cups borax

2 cups washing soda

2 cups baking soda

1 cup OxiClean

50 drops lavender essential oil

TO MAKE: Using a food processor or a hand cheese grater, grate the bar of soap. Then combine all ingredients in a large bucket. Mix well.

TO USE: Save the scoop from the jar of OxiClean to use to add laundry soap to washing machine. Use 1 scoop for a normal load or 2 scoops for a large load. This recipe is safe for HE machines; just place the soap in the drum of the machine before adding clothes.

TO STORE: Store indefinitely in large covered container the soap was mixed in, or a smaller container, on your laundry room shelf. Refill the smaller container from the larger container as needed.

NO-GRATE LAUNDRY SOAP

If grating soap isn't your thing, try this No-Grate Laundry Soap that uses tea tree and rosemary essential oils to purify and cleanse.

YIELD: 1 gallon

3 tablespoons washing soda

3 tablespoons borax

3 tablespoons liquid Castile soap

4 cups boiling water, plus cold water to fill jug

10 drops tea tree essential oil

10 drops rosemary essential oil

TO MAKE: Combine washing soda and borax in a 1-gallon jug. Pour in Castile soap and boiling water. Shake well. Next, fill jug to the top with cold water. Add tea tree and rosemary essential oils and swirl around to mix.

TO USE: Use ½ cup per load. Launder as usual.

TO STORE: Store indefinitely in 1-gallon jug.

SENSITIVE SKIN LAVENDER LAUNDRY SOAP

For sensitive skin, try this all-natural laundry soap with minimal ingredients. It is nontoxic and fragranced with lavender essential oil to give your laundry the lightest scent. It's perfect for getting your clothes clean without the chance of irritation.

YIELD: 7 cups

1 bar Castile soap

3 cups washing soda

3 cups baking soda

20 drops lavender essential oil

TO MAKE: Using a food processor or a hand cheese grater, grate the bar of soap. Then combine all ingredients in a bucket. Mix well.

TO USE: Use ¼–½ cup of detergent per load, depending on load size. This recipe is safe for HE machines; just place the soap in the drum of the machine before adding clothes.

TO STORE: Store indefinitely in large covered container the soap was mixed in, or a smaller container, on your laundry room shelf. Refill the smaller container from the larger container as needed.

HOMEMADE LIQUID LAUNDRY SOAP

This eco-friendly, nontoxic laundry soap is easy to mix up and costs pennies per load! It uses tea tree and lemon essential oils to purify and lift stains.

YIELD: Approximately 5 gallons

1 bar Fels-Naptha soap

4 cups water

5 gallons hot water

1 cup washing soda

1 cup borax

1 cup baking soda

20 drops tea tree essential oil

20 drops lemon essential oil

TO MAKE: Using a food processor or a hand cheese grater, grate the bar of soap. Add to a pot on the stove with 4 cups of water over medium heat. Stir until soap is completely melted, then remove from heat. Fill a 5-gallon bucket halfway to the top with hot water. Add in soap mixture, washing soda, borax, and baking soda. Mix well. Add in tea tree and lemon essential oils. Fill the rest of the way up with hot water and stir. Place lid on bucket and allow to sit for 24 hours. Stir and add to smaller bottles if desired.

TO USE: Use ¼–½ cup of detergent for each load. Launder as usual.

TO STORE: Store indefinitely in covered containers.

BORAX-FREE LEMON LAUNDRY DETERGENT

Feel confident that you are using the purest detergent possible with this nontoxic laundry detergent recipe. Lemon essential oil cuts through dirt and grime, and purifies in the process!

YIELD: 103 ounces

3 bars Castile soap

1 (55-ounce) box washing soda

1 (3-pound) container OxiClean Versatile Stain Remover Free

30 drops lemon essential oil

TO MAKE: Using a food processor or a hand cheese grater, grate the bars of soap. Then combine all ingredients in a large container with a lid. Mix well.

TO USE: Use 2 tablespoons detergent per load. Launder as usual.

TO STORE: Store indefinitely in a covered container in a cool, dark place.

TIP To remove any remaining soap from clothing and get your clothes as clean as possible, use the Lavender and Lemon Fabric Softener found in this chapter.

LIQUID SOAP NUTS

Soap nuts, a berry shell that naturally contains soap, are the perfect all-natural laundry detergent. Use this recipe to turn them into liquid to use in your HE washing machine. Lavender essential oil adds a a light scent to your laundry.

YIELD: 4 cups

40 soap nuts

4 cups water

20 drops lavender essential oil

TO MAKE: Add soap nuts to water in a pot on the stove and bring to a boil. Allow to simmer for 1 hour. Remove from heat and cool to room temperature. Once cool, stir in lavender essential oil.

TO USE: Add 2–3 tablespoons of Liquid Soap Nuts to each load of laundry. Launder as usual.

TO STORE: Store indefinitely in a covered container.

LAUNDRY BOMBS

Making and using "bombs" in your laundry is a fun and inexpensive way to get the job done. Lemon and lavender essential oils provide a scent explosion that brings extra cleansing powers! Use these Laundry Bombs in place of your normal laundry detergent.

YIELD: 20–30 Laundry Bombs

½ bar Castile soap (lavender-scented soap is a great choice)

1½ cups washing soda

2 tablespoons Epsom salts

3 tablespoons hydrogen peroxide

¼ cup plus 2 tablespoons vinegar, divided

10 drops lavender essential oil

10 drops lemon essential oil

1-ounce silicone molds or ice cube trays

2 tablespoons distilled water

TO MAKE: Grate Castile soap into a large bowl using a food processor or a hand cheese grater. Add in washing soda and Epsom salts. Mix well. Slowly pour in hydrogen peroxide and ¼ cup vinegar. Stir together. Add lavender and lemon essential oils. Place in molds or use a rounded scoop to place scoops on parchment paper–covered cookie sheet. Combine the remaining 2 tablespoons of vinegar and water in a small spray bottle. Spritz Laundry Bombs with water-vinegar mixture. Let sit for a few hours until hardened, then place in a covered jar or container.

TO USE: Drop 1 Laundry Bomb into your washing machine and launder as usual.

TO STORE: Store indefinitely in covered container in a cool, dark place.

CLOTH DIAPER DETERGENT

Know exactly what you're washing your baby's diapers in by making your own all-natural detergent at home! Lemon essential oil will keep things fresh and clean while purifying, cleansing, and adding extra whitening power.

YIELD: 6 cups

2 cups washing soda

2 cups baking soda

2 cups OxiClean

20 drops lemon essential oil

TO MAKE: Combine all ingredients in a large container or jar with a lid. Mix well.

TO USE: Add 1–2 tablespoons of detergent to your laundry. Launder as usual.

TO STORE: Store indefinitely in covered container.

LAVENDER AND LEMON FABRIC SOFTENER

Vinegar is the perfect fabric softener. It is all-natural and works as well as any commercial product, without harmful chemicals. Lavender and lemon essential oils create a fresh, clean scent that lasts!

YIELD: 2 cups

2 cups vinegar

15 drops lavender essential oil

15 drops lemon essential oil

TO MAKE: Combine all ingredients in a bottle with a lid. Shake well.

TO USE: Fill your rinse-agent cup in your washing machine with this fabric softener as normal.

TO STORE: Store indefinitely in covered bottle.

ROSEMARY AND LAVENDER DRAWER SACHETS

Leave a lasting scent on your clothes by using these easy-to-make and cost-effective drawer sachets! Place one in each drawer or hang one in your closet for a refreshing experience.

YIELD: 8 sachets

2 cups dried lavender buds

10 drops rosemary essential oil

15 drops lavender essential oil

8 small muslin drawstring bags

TO MAKE: Add lavender buds to a large bowl. Add rosemary and lavender essential oils. Mix well. Add 4 tablespoons of lavender mixture to each muslin bag. Close each drawstring bag.

TO USE: Add to drawers and closets.

TO STORE: Refresh sachets with essential oils with 3–4 drops of your favorite essential oil approximately every 2 weeks or as needed.

TIP Add one of these sachets to your off-season clothes you're storing to keep things fresh.

FABRIC REFRESHER SPRAY

Freshen laundry that's been hanging in the closet a little too long with this Fabric Refresher Spray. Lemongrass essential oil removes odors and leaves a fresh, lasting scent!

YIELD: ½ cup

½ cup distilled water

15 drops lemongrass essential oil

TO MAKE: Combine water and lemongrass essential oil in a spray bottle. Shake well.

TO USE: Spray lightly on garment to freshen.

TO STORE: Store indefinitely in spray bottle.

FORGOTTEN LAUNDRY FRESHENER

We've all forgotten a load of laundry in the washer a time or two. Try this DIY method of removing that stinky laundry smell by using tea tree, lemon, lime, and pine essential oils to purify your clothes!

YIELD: ½ cup, or 1 application of Forgotten Laundry Refresher

½ cup vinegar

2 drops each tea tree, lemon, lime, and pine essential oils

TO MAKE: Combine vinegar and essential oils and mix well.

TO USE: Wash clothes again with your normal detergent, this time adding Forgotten Laundry Freshener to your rinse cycle.

MUSTY SMELL REMOVER

Left your wet laundry in the washer too long? Don't let musty clothes get you down. Get rid of mold and mildew spores the natural way with tea tree essential oil!

YIELD: 1 cup

1 cup vinegar

20 drops tea tree essential oil

1 cup baking soda

TO MAKE: Combine vinegar and tea tree essential oil in a dish. Add baking soda to a small bowl. Pour in vinegar mixture and mix well.

TO USE: Add clothes to washer. Set your machine to the hottest water setting. Add your normal amount of detergent. Add in Musty Smell Remover. Allow to agitate 3 minutes. Stop washer and allow to sit for 30 minutes. Turn back on to complete washing cycle.

TIP Use a vinegar rinse such as the Lavender and Lemon Fabric Softener in this chapter to get clothes extra clean and fresh.

ALL-NATURAL BLEACH ALTERNATIVE

Regular commercial bleach can be harmful to your skin, lungs, and even your septic system. Use this All-Natural Bleach Alternative with lemon essential oil to whiten whites the natural way!

YIELD: 16 cups

1¾ cups hydrogen peroxide

¼ cup lemon juice

1 tablespoon citric acid

20 drops lemon essential oil

1 gallon distilled water

TO MAKE: Add hydrogen peroxide, lemon juice, citric acid, and lemon essential oil to the bottom of a 1-gallon jug. Mix well by giving it a gentle shake. Fill the rest of the container up with water and shake to combine.

TO USE: Add 1 cup of bleach alternative to laundry as usual.

TO STORE: Store for up to 1 month in 1-gallon container in a cool, dark place.

ALL-NATURAL OXICLEAN SUBSTITUTE FOR LIGHT-COLORED CLOTHES

Light-colored clothes that need whitening and brightening can benefit from this recipe. Make your own laundry-boosting and whitening OxiClean at home whenever you need to brighten clothes and remove laundry stains. Lemon essential oil gives it extra whitening and stain-lifting power! Keep in mind that this recipe is for light-colored clothes; the recipe could lighten dark-colored clothing.

YIELD: 1½ cups, or 1 application of All-Natural OxiClean Substitute for Light-Colored Clothes

1 cup distilled water

½ cup hydrogen peroxide

½ cup washing soda

10 drops lemon essential oil

TO MAKE: In a large jar with a lid or a large spray bottle, combine water, hydrogen peroxide, washing soda, and lemon essential oil. Shake well.

TO USE: Pour or spray onto stain. Allow to sit for 30 minutes or overnight. Launder as usual.

LAUNDRY BRIGHTENER

Brighten both your whites and your colors with this lemony Laundry Brightener. Lemon essential oil mixed with lemon juice gives this product its extra whitening power.

YIELD: 1 cup, or 1 application of Laundry Brightener

1 cup lemon juice

10 drops lemon essential oil

TO MAKE: Combine lemon juice and lemon essential oil in a cup. Mix well.

TO USE: Add Laundry Brightener to your wash cycle along with your regular detergent. Wash as normal.

TIP Add Lavender and Lemon Fabric Softener found in this chapter to your rinse cycle to brighten and freshen further!

ALL-NATURAL LAVENDER DRYER SHEETS

Use this recipe to create your own lavender dryer sheets that can be used again and again! Lavender essential oil will leave your clothes smelling great, and tea tree essential oil will cleanse and purify every time.

YIELD: 20 dryer sheets

1 cup vinegar

5 drops lavender essential oil

5 drops tea tree essential oil

20 (4" × 4") fabric squares cut from old T-shirts, washrags, or flour sack towels

TO MAKE: Combine vinegar and essential oils in a covered jar. Mix well. Add in fabric squares and cover. Flip over the jar and allow the mixture to soak into the fabric.

TO USE: Remove 1 dryer sheet from jar and squeeze out excess solution. Throw into dryer and use as you would normally use a dryer sheet.

TO STORE: Store for up to 1 month in covered container.

EASY DRYER CLOTH

Freshen your laundry and remove static cling with this easy-to-make dryer cloth. Use your favorite essential oil each time you do laundry to add a pleasing scent.

YIELD: 1 dryer cloth

½ cup vinegar

½ cup distilled water

2-4 drops essential oil of choice (try lavender, lemon, or grapefruit)

1 washcloth

TO MAKE: Combine vinegar, water, and essential oil in a bowl. Mix well. Add washcloth to bowl. Remove and squeeze out excess water mixture.

TO USE: Add wet washcloth to dryer with wet clothes. Dry as usual.

THREE-INGREDIENT FABRIC SOFTENER CRYSTALS

Making your own fabric softener crystals is satisfying and easy on your budget! This is a great way to soften and purify your clothes and add a fresh scent with lavender and rosemary essential oils.

YIELD: 4 cups

4 cups Epsom salts

20 drops lavender essential oil

20 drops rosemary essential oil

TO MAKE: Combine Epsom salts and essential oils in a large bowl. Mix well.

TO USE: Add 1–2 tablespoons of crystals to washing machine along with your laundry detergent. Wash as normal.

TO STORE: Store indefinitely in a covered container.

STATIC CLING REMOVER

Remove static cling while freshening your clothes with this simple DIY recipe! Add your favorite essential oil for a light scent that freshens your clothes while removing static cling.

YIELD: 1 packet

4 tablespoons Himalayan rock salt

10 drops essential oil of choice (lavender, lemon, rosemary, and grapefruit are great choices)

Small cotton drawstring bag (search for "spice bags" on *www.amazon .com*)

TO MAKE: Combine rock salt and chosen essential oil in a bowl. Mix well. Place mixture in cotton bag. Tie well to close.

TO USE: Add to dryer with wet clothes. Run dryer as normal.

TO STORE: Store indefinitely in laundry area and reuse with next laundry cycle. Refresh essential oils as needed when scent fades.

LEMON-SCENTED WOOL DRYER BALLS

Wool dryer balls are a great way to cut drying time and soften laundry at the same time. Lemon essential oil freshens things up, too!

YIELD: 1 application

1-2 drops lemon essential oil per wool dryer ball

6 wool dryer balls (can be found on www.amazon.com or www.etsy.com)

TO MAKE: Add 1–2 drops lemon essential oil to each dryer ball.

TO USE: Add 4–6 wool dryer balls to dryer with wet clothes. Run as normal.

TO STORE: Store dryer balls near dryer for future use. Refresh essential oil with each use.

SPRAY STARCH

Remove the chemicals from this laundry must-have for perfectly pressed shirts! Lemon and rosemary essential oils leave a fresh scent on your clothes that lasts all day.

YIELD: 1 cup

1 cup hot distilled water

1 tablespoon cornstarch

6 drops lemon essential oil

6 drops rosemary essential oil

TO MAKE: Combine hot water and cornstarch in a covered jar. Shake well until cornstarch is dissolved. Add in lemon and rosemary essential oils. Transfer to a spray bottle.

TO USE: Shake bottle and then spray on clothes before ironing.

TO STORE: Store indefinitely in spray bottle.

LAVENDER-FRESH WRINKLE RELEASER

Don't waste money on store-bought wrinkle releasers when you can make your own at home and personalize them with any scent you like! This recipe with lavender and lemon essential oils leaves your clothes wrinkle-free and smelling fresh.

YIELD: 1 cup

½ cup vinegar

½ cup distilled water

10 drops lavender essential oil

10 drops lemon essential oil

TO MAKE: Add vinegar, water, and essential oils to a spray bottle. Shake well.

TO USE: Lightly mist clothing with wrinkle releaser. Use hands to smooth out fabric. Hang to dry.

TO STORE: Store indefinitely in spray bottle.

LEMONGRASS LINEN MIST

Lemongrass is one of the most uplifting scents there is. Add some "happy" to your day by adding a spray of Lemongrass Linen Mist to your clothes, sheets, and towels.

YIELD: ½ cup

½ cup distilled water

20 drops lemongrass essential oil

TO MAKE: Combine water and lemongrass essential oil in a spray bottle with a fine-mist spray top. Shake well.

TO USE: Shake bottle before each use. Spray on clothes, sheets, towels, curtains, and anywhere else you'd like an extra-fresh scent!

TO STORE: Store indefinitely in spray bottle.

PILLOW CLEANER

Think your bed pillows can't be washed? They can! Get them clean with this easy DIY recipe that uses tea tree essential oil to purify and freshen.

YIELD: ¾ cup, or 1 application of Pillow Cleaner

¼ cup laundry detergent (use one of the recipes in this chapter for best results)

½ cup vinegar

20 drops tea tree essential oil

TO USE: Place 2–3 pillows in your washer. Add detergent as normal. Add vinegar and tea tree essential oil to your rinse cycle. Wash with hot water. Add an extra rinse to get out all soap and get pillows extra clean.

TIP   When running your pillows through the dryer, use one of the dryer sheet recipes in this chapter and a few tennis balls to keep pillows fluffy.

STEAM IRON CLEANER

Keep your iron in good working condition with the help of tea tree essential oil. This DIY method is easy and sure to have your iron working like new in no time!

YIELD: 1 application of Steam Iron Cleaner

Enough vinegar to fill ¼ of your iron water reservoir

2-3 drops tea tree essential oil

Enough water to fill ¾ of your iron water reservoir

TO MAKE: Add enough vinegar to fill your steam iron water reservoir ¼ of the way full. Add in tea tree essential oil, then add enough water to fill the reservoir the rest of the way.

TO USE: Turn your iron on high steam. Iron a clean cloth until the vinegar and water mixture is gone. Then fill with clean water and iron a clean cloth again.

TOP-LOAD WASHING MACHINE CLEANER

You may not think about it, but your washing machine needs a good cleaning from time to time! Use this nontoxic method to get it clean the easy way. The addition of tea tree and lemon essential oils helps get rid of grime and dirt and removes odors!

YIELD: 1 application of Top-Load Washing Machine Cleaner

1 cup baking soda

3 cups vinegar

20 drops tea tree essential oil

20 drops lemon essential oil

TO USE: Set your washing machine to the hottest temperature possible and allow to fill. Once full, add baking soda, vinegar, and essential oils to the water. Agitate for a few minutes, then stop the machine and allow the mixture to sit for 30 minutes to an hour. While it's soaking, use a small scrub brush and cloth and clean around the inside of the washing machine and lid. Once time is up, close the lid and allow the cycle to continue as normal. Once complete, run a hot-water rinse cycle. Clean away any grime or gunk left over. Leave the lid open to dry out washing machine completely.

HE WASHING MACHINE CLEANER

Washing machines get full of grime and dirt, and you need to clean them to keep them running at full potential. If you have an HE machine, this is easily done with the "clean washer" setting using nontoxic cleaning products such as this cleaner with tea tree and lemon essential oils!

YIELD: 1 application of HE Washing Machine Cleaner

20 drops tea tree essential oil

20 drops lemon essential oil

1 cup vinegar

1 cup baking soda

TO MAKE: Combine essential oils and vinegar in a cup. Mix well.

TO USE: Add baking soda to drum of machine and close door. Add vinegar mixture to the bleach cup of your machine. Turn machine to "clean washer" setting and add an extra rinse to the cycle. Clean as normal. Once the cycle is complete, open the door and wipe down the inside of the door and along the rubber gasket. Leave the door open to dry washing machine completely.

TIP Always use a vinegar fabric softener rinse (like the Lavender and Lemon Fabric Softener in this chapter) in your HE washing machine to keep it as clean and gunk-free as possible. Also, always leave the door of your machine open to air-dry completely in order to keep mold and mildew away.

GUM AND GREASE REMOVER

Remove gum and grease from laundry with ease! Workhorse lemon essential oil is known to remove sticky, greasy messes the easy way.

YIELD: 1 application of Gum and Grease Remover

Lemon essential oil, as needed

TO MAKE: Add 1–3 drops of lemon essential oil to gum or grease stain.

TO USE: Rub in well. Remove gum if present. Launder as usual.

LEMON ALL-PURPOSE STAIN REMOVER

This all-purpose stain remover is easy to make and budget-friendly! Lemon essential oil helps break down the stain to remove it every time.

YIELD: 1 application of Lemon All-Purpose Stain Remover

3-4 drops lemon essential oil

1 bar Fels-Naptha soap or your favorite brand of soap that is known to remove stains

TO USE: As soon as you can, apply the lemon essential oil to the stain. Next, wet the end of the bar soap and rub over the stain. Allow to sit for 5 minutes before laundering.

COFFEE STAIN REMOVER

Clean coffee stains easily with this all-natural method. Lemon essential oil is known to break down stains with ease!

YIELD: 1 application of Coffee Stain Remover

Lemon essential oil, as needed

Vinegar, as needed

TO USE: Apply several drops of lemon essential oil to stain and rub in. Soak in vinegar for 1 hour before laundering.

WINE STAIN REMOVER

Red wine stains can be a pain to remove. Use this fuss-free method to remove them with the help of club soda and lemon essential oil.

YIELD: 1 application of Wine Stain Remover

1 cup club soda

5 drops lemon essential oil

TO MAKE: Combine club soda and lemon essential oil in a small bowl. Mix well.

TO USE: Rinse stain with mixture. Blot with a clean cloth to remove the stain. Repeat until stain is removed.

GRASS STAIN REMOVER

Grass stains are inevitable if you're passionate about gardening or if you have kids around. Try this all-natural method of removing grass stains with lemon essential oil, which is known to break up those hard-to-remove stains.

YIELD: 1½ cups, or 1 application of Grass Stain Remover

1 cup hydrogen peroxide

½ cup liquid Castile soap

10 drops lemon essential oil

TO MAKE: Combine hydrogen peroxide, soap, and lemon essential oil in a spray bottle. Shake well.

TO USE: Soak stain with mixture and rub in. Allow to sit for 1 hour, then launder as usual.

INK STAIN REMOVER

An ink stain doesn't have to mean the end of a garment's life! Use this trick with lemon essential oil to get your clothes as good as new.

YIELD: 1 application of Ink Stain Remover

1-2 drops lemon essential oil

1-2 tablespoons rubbing alcohol

3-4 drops liquid dish soap (such as Lavender Dish Soap in Chapter 4)

TO USE: Apply 1–2 drops of lemon essential oil to the ink stain and rub in. Next, pour rubbing alcohol over the stain. Blot well with a paper towel. Then add dish soap and rub into the stain well. Allow to sit for 30 minutes and launder as usual.

CHAPTER 7

Kid and Pet Areas

Using essential oils in the areas in which your kids and pets spend most of their time is a great way to remove toxins, provide eco-friendly solutions, and save money! This chapter will teach you how to clean your children's and pets' spaces from top to bottom while providing soothing and relaxing benefits. Throughout this chapter, you'll find lavender, lemon, orange, tea tree, and peppermint essential oils used most often. All of these oils are great for purifying and cleansing the all-natural way and provide a pleasant scent in the process. You'll also learn how to make some toxin-free, healthy, super fun toys that your kids will return to again and again. So don't hesitate to make Toy Surprise Bath Bombs, Super Soft Playdough, Cloth Diaper–Safe Diaper Cream, and more. Everything you find in this chapter is guaranteed to make your children's and pets' spaces green and clean!

ONE-INGREDIENT HAND PURIFIER

It doesn't get much easier than this! This One-Ingredient Hand Purifier made with lemon essential oil is perfect for when you're on the go and there's no water in sight. Lemon's cleansing properties make it the perfect way to get hands clean quickly.

YIELD: 1 application of One-Ingredient Hand Purifier

2-3 drops lemon essential oil

TO USE: Apply 2–3 drops of lemon essential oil to hands. Rub thoroughly until essential oil has been absorbed into skin.

HAND CLEANSING LOTION

This Hand Cleansing Lotion will cleanse without drying out your hands. With the purifying properties of tea tree essential oil, this recipe is the perfect addition to your purse, diaper bag, or kids' backpacks.

YIELD: Approximately ½ cup

5 tablespoons aloe vera gel

4 tablespoons distilled water

¼ teaspoon vitamin E oil

5 drops lemon essential oil

5 drops tea tree essential oil

TO MAKE: Combine aloe, water, vitamin E oil, and essential oils in a bowl. Mix well. Transfer mixture to a small squeeze bottle and shake well.

TO USE: Apply a dime-sized amount to hands and rub thoroughly until lotion has been absorbed into skin.

TO STORE: Store indefinitely in squeeze bottle.

HAND PURIFYING SPRAY

Reach for this Hand Purifying Spray anytime you need a fast cleanse on the go. Dirt and grime on hands, doorknobs, and even shopping carts are no match for this spray made with tea tree, lemon, and lavender essential oils. Coconut oil helps keep your hands moisturized, too.

YIELD: 4 (2-ounce) spray bottles

½ cup distilled water

¼ cup witch hazel

¼ cup fractionated coconut oil

10 drops tea tree essential oil

10 drops lavender essential oil

10 drops lemon essential oil

TO MAKE: Combine all ingredients in a bowl. Mix well. Using a funnel, pour into 4 (2-ounce) spray bottles.

TO USE: Spray on hands, rub thoroughly until spray has been absorbed into skin, and let air-dry.

TO STORE: Store indefinitely in spray bottles.

LIQUID HAND SANITIZER

Forget chemical-filled, store-bought hand sanitizers. Use this all-natural version to remove dirt and grime, and cleanse your hands without toxic ingredients. Lavender and lemon essential oils work well together to sanitize and freshen, making them the perfect combination for this recipe!

YIELD: Approximately ½ cup

5 tablespoons pure aloe vera gel

1 tablespoon witch hazel

3 tablespoons distilled water

10 drops lemon essential oil

10 drops lavender essential oil

TO MAKE: Combine all ingredients in a bowl. Mix well. Transfer mixture to small squeeze bottles and shake well.

TO USE: Apply a dime-sized amount to hands and rub thoroughly until sanitizer has been absorbed by skin.

TO STORE: Store indefinitely in squeeze bottles.

ALL-NATURAL TOY CLEANSER

Get rid of dirt and grime on all your kids' toys without chemicals! This All-Natural Toy Cleanser with tea tree and lemon essential oils is safe to use around kids and will purify with ease.

YIELD: 1 cup

½ cup vinegar

½ cup distilled water

20 drops tea tree essential oil

20 drops lemon essential oil

TO MAKE: Combine all ingredients in a spray bottle. Shake well.

TO USE: Spray toys to be cleansed and wipe if desired. Allow to dry. No need to rinse.

TO STORE: Store indefinitely in spray bottle.

PACIFIER PURIFIER

The last thing you want to do is clean your baby's pacifier with harsh chemicals that he could ingest. Fortunately, this all-natural solution made with tea tree essential oil will safely cleanse and keep your baby safe and sound.

YIELD: ½ cup

¼ cup distilled water

¼ cup vinegar

1 teaspoon liquid Castile soap

5 drops tea tree essential oil

TO MAKE: Combine all ingredients in a small spray bottle. Shake well.

TO USE: Spray pacifier to be cleaned with solution. Let sit for a couple of minutes. Wipe off any dirt and rinse well with hot water.

TO STORE: Store indefinitely in spray bottle.

KID-FRIENDLY CLEANSING WIPES

Kids love to get dirty, and they love to help clean things! Give them one of these Kid-Friendly Cleansing Wipes to get both hands and soft and hard toys purified. Lavender and lemon essential oils ensure that dirt and grime are a thing of the past.

YIELD: 1 roll of wipes

1 roll high-quality paper towels

2 cups distilled water

1 tablespoon liquid Castile soap

1 tablespoon fractionated coconut oil

10 drops lavender essential oil

10 drops lemon essential oil

TO MAKE: Lay the paper towel roll horizontally on the table in front of you, then use a serrated knife to cut the roll in half. Use one half of roll now and keep one half of roll for next use. Next, combine water, soap, coconut oil, and essential oils in a small bowl. Mix well. Remove the cardboard tube from the paper towel roll and discard, then place paper towel roll half in a plastic container (like an empty baby wipes container). Pour the water mixture over the paper towels and allow to sit for an hour.

TO USE: Pull wipes from the center of the roll and use to clean hands or wash face, or as diaper cleansing wipes.

TO STORE: Store for up to 1 month in container.

VARIATION

Go green by buying cloth wipes, cutting up an old T-shirt, or using washcloths instead of paper towels.

DIAPER PAIL FRESHENER

Diaper pails can get stinky! Absorb odors and freshen up with these diaper pail freshening disks made with baking soda and lemon essential oil. The same fresheners used in your kitchen are safe to use in your nursery as well.

YIELD: 16 disks

1 cup baking soda

¼ cup distilled water

10 drops lemon essential oil

1-ounce silicone molds or ice cube trays

TO MAKE: Combine baking soda, water, and essential oil in a bowl. Pour into molds and allow to harden uncovered for 24 hours or more.

TO USE: Place 1 disk in the bottom of the diaper pail to remove odors and freshen. Replace every 30 days.

TO STORE: Store indefinitely in covered container or jar in a cool, dark place.

ROOM DEODORIZER SPRAY

Freshen kids' spaces with this all-natural room deodorizer that can be personalized with your favorite essential oils! This version uses lemon and lime essential oils to purify the air, remove odors, and provide an uplifting, citrusy scent.

YIELD: ¼ cup

¼ cup distilled water

10 drops lavender essential oil

10 drops lime essential oil

TO MAKE: Combine water and essential oils in a small spray bottle. Shake well.

TO USE: Thoroughly spray room whenever a fresh scent is needed.

TO STORE: Store indefinitely in spray bottle.

HOMEMADE ORANGE OXYGENATED CLEANER

From marker-stained carpets and toys to juice-stained onesies, this homemade oxygenated cleaner is the answer! Orange essential oil cuts through dirt and stains easily, is safe for use around kids, and does its job naturally.

YIELD: 1 cup, or 1 application of Homemade Orange Oxygenated Cleaner

½ cup distilled water

¼ cup hydrogen peroxide

¼ cup washing soda

10 drops orange essential oil

TO MAKE: Combine all ingredients in a large jar with a lid or a large spray bottle. Shake well.

TO USE: Pour or spray onto stain. Allow to sit for 30 minutes or overnight. Launder as usual.

CRAYON AND PERMANENT MARKER STAIN REMOVER

If you have kids, you're bound to have crayon and permanent marker stains somewhere you'd rather not at one time or another! Luckily, lemon essential oil works hard to break down these stains on hard surfaces in no time.

YIELD: 1 application of Crayon and Permanent Marker Stain Remover

3-4 drops lemon essential oil

1 Mr. Clean Magic Eraser

TO MAKE: Apply lemon essential oil to stain.

TO USE: Rub in well and allow to sit for several minutes to dissolve stain. Next, use a Magic Eraser to rub the marker stain until it comes completely clean. If it's a big job, you may have to apply the lemon essential oil more than once, but keep at it—it will come off!

STICKER REMOVER

Remove sticky residue from stickers and labels with this easy trick! The lemon essential oil will break down the glue and allow you to remove the sticky mess with ease.

YIELD: 1 application of Sticker Remover

1-2 drops lemon essential oil

TO MAKE: Apply 1–2 drops of lemon essential oil to sticker or label to be removed.

TO USE: Rub in well. Use a lint-free cloth to wipe off the sticky residue. Repeat until completely clean.

DRY-ERASE MARKER REMOVER

Ever have leftover dry-erase marker on your boards? Or worse, on your walls? Remove it naturally with lemon essential oil! Lemon is great for cutting through the ingredients found in dry-erase markers and getting your surfaces clean.

YIELD: ½ cup

½ cup distilled water

20 drops lemon essential oil

TO MAKE: Combine water and lemon essential oil in a small spray bottle. Shake well.

TO USE: Apply to surface to be cleaned. Wipe with a dry cloth.

TO STORE: Store indefinitely in small spray bottle.

TOY SURPRISE BATH BOMBS

Add a little fun into bath time with these bath bombs that reveal a toy as they fizz in the tub! Essential oils add a scent explosion to make the experience even better.

YIELD: 6–8 bath bombs

1¾ cups baking soda

1 cup citric acid

2 cups cornstarch

Distilled water, as needed

Food coloring (optional)

10 drops essential oil of choice (lavender, lemon, and orange are great choices)

60-millimeter silicone molds or bath bomb molds

6-8 (1"–2") plastic toy figures

TO MAKE: Slowly sift baking soda, citric acid, and cornstarch through a sieve to remove larger chunks, or use a fork to mash into a fine powder. Fill a small bottle with distilled water and lightly spritz the mixture. Add in a couple of drops of food coloring if you'd like to color your bath bombs. Mix well until the mixture becomes the consistency of sand that can be molded with your hands. Add in your chosen essential oil and mix well. Transfer the mixture to silicone molds or bath bomb molds. To add in a toy, fill the mold halfway, add toy, and continue to fill with mixture. Allow to harden for a few hours to overnight before removing.

TO USE: Pop 1 bath bomb into your bath water and enjoy watching the plastic toy reveal itself as the bath bomb melts away.

TO STORE: Store indefinitely in a covered container or jar in a cool, dark place.

SLEEPY TIME BATH BOMBS

Get your child ready for dreamland with one of these calming lavender and orange bath bombs. These essential oils are known to relax both the mind and body, making them the perfect choice for this bedtime bath bomb.

YIELD: 6–8 bath bombs

1¾ cups baking soda

1 cup citric acid

2 cups cornstarch

1 tablespoon fractionated coconut oil or almond oil

Distilled water, as needed

Purple food coloring (optional)

10 drops lavender essential oil

10 drops orange essential oil

60-millimeter silicone molds or bath bomb molds

TO MAKE: Slowly sift baking soda, citric acid, and cornstarch through a sieve to remove larger chunks, or use a fork to mash into a fine powder. Add in coconut or almond oil and mix well with a fork. Fill a small spray bottle with distilled water and add food coloring if desired. Lightly spritz the mixture with water. Mix well until the mixture becomes the consistency of sand that can be molded with your hands. Add in essential oils and mix well. Transfer the mixture to silicone molds or bath bomb molds. Allow to harden uncovered for a few hours or overnight before removing.

TO USE: Pop 1 bath bomb into your child's bath water before bedtime.

TO STORE: Store indefinitely in a covered container or jar in a cool, dark place.

BATH FIZZIES

Bath Fizzies are a great way to add a little extra fun to your child's bath while moisturizing skin at the same time! Lavender essential oil works to smooth and nourish skin naturally.

YIELD: 12–16 Bath Fizzies

1¾ cups baking soda

½ cup citric acid

½ cup Epsom salts

1 tablespoon fractionated coconut oil or almond oil

1 tablespoon olive oil

1 tablespoon distilled water

10 drops lavender essential oil

2-ounce silicone molds or bath bomb molds

TO MAKE: Slowly sift baking soda and citric acid through a sieve to remove larger chunks, or use a fork to mash into a fine powder. Mix in Epsom salts. Next, add in coconut or almond oil and mix well with a fork. Slowly mix in olive oil and water until the mixture becomes the consistency of sand that can be molded with your hands. Add in lavender essential oil and mix well. Transfer the mixture to molds and allow to harden uncovered for a few hours before removing.

TO USE: Pop 1 bath bomb into your child's bath water and enjoy!

TO STORE: Store indefinitely in a covered container or jar in a cool, dark place.

SCENTED BUBBLES

Mix up your own bubble solution easily and more affordably than those you can buy at the store. Scent the bubbles with your favorite essential oil for a fun and uplifting bubble-blowing experience!

YIELD: 1 cup

1 cup hot water

1 tablespoon white sugar

2 tablespoons liquid Castile soap

1 tablespoon vegetable glycerin

5-10 drops essential oil of choice (lavender, lemon, and orange are great choices)

TO MAKE: Combine water and sugar in a jar. Mix well. Add in soap, glycerin, and your chosen essential oil.

TO USE: Use bubble wands or pipe cleaners to form shapes and use with bubble solution.

TO STORE: Store in a covered jar up to 1 month.

UPLIFTING BUBBLE BATH

Make your own nontoxic bubble bath for your kids with this DIY recipe! This recipe is easy to make and can be made again and again once you purchase the initial ingredients. The orange essential oil provides a nice uplifting scent while soothing your children's skin.

YIELD: 1½ cups

1 cup distilled water

½ cup liquid Castile soap

2 teaspoons vegetable glycerin

10 drops orange essential oil

TO MAKE: Combine all ingredients in a jar or container with a lid. Mix well.

TO USE: Give the bubble bath mixture a little shake before adding ⅛–¼ cup to running bath water.

TO STORE: Store indefinitely in covered jar or container.

CALMING BUBBLE BATH

Help your child relax and get ready for a good night's rest with this Calming Bubble Bath. Lavender and coconut oils provide the best bubble bath experience before bed!

YIELD: 1½ cups

1 cup distilled water

½ cup liquid Castile soap

2 teaspoons vegetable glycerin

10 drops lavender essential oil

1 tablespoon fractionated coconut oil

TO MAKE: Combine all ingredients in a jar or container with a lid. Mix well.

TO USE: Give the bubble bath mixture a little shake before adding ⅛–¼ cup to running bath water.

TO STORE: Store indefinitely in covered jar or container.

SOOTHING CHEST RUB

If your little one is congested and stuffy, don't reach for chemical-filled rubs. This Soothing Chest Rub is safe to use and contains a variety of essential oils that are known to relieve stuffiness. Try rubbing it on your child's chest, back, or feet—it's sure to help!

YIELD: ¼ cup

¼ cup coconut oil

1 tablespoon beeswax pastilles

5 drops eucalyptus essential oil

5 drops rosemary essential oil (omit for children under 2 years old)

5 drops lavender essential oil

TO MAKE: Melt together coconut oil and beeswax in a small pot on medium heat. Stir until smooth. Remove from heat and allow to cool for 5–10 minutes. Add in essential oils and mix well. Pour into a small jar with a lid and allow to harden for 30–45 minutes before use.

TO USE: Rub mixture on chest, back, or feet as needed. Make sure to cover feet with socks to keep little hands from getting the rub in their eyes or mouth.

TO STORE: Store indefinitely in small jar with lid.

CALMING AROMATHERAPY MOONSAND

Kids love moonsand! It's not playdough or sand but a combination of both! Moonsand is soft and squishy, and can be used again and again. Make your own at home with all-natural ingredients like lavender essential oil, which provides a relaxing sensory experience due to its aromatherapy benefits.

YIELD: 8 cups

8 cups flour

1 cup coconut oil, melted

30 drops lavender essential oil

TO MAKE: Combine flour and coconut oil in a large container. Mix with a pastry dough blender until combined. Add lavender essential oil and mix well.

TO USE: Use fun tools and toys to play in the sand and mold creations.

TO STORE: Store indefinitely in a covered container.

UPLIFTING MOONSAND

Uplift and energize your child with this citrusy moonsand. Easy to make and all-natural, Uplifting Moonsand is the perfect rainy day activity!

YIELD: 8 cups

8 cups flour

1 cup vegetable oil

15 drops lemon essential oil

15 drops orange essential oil

TO MAKE: Combine flour and vegetable oil in a large container. Mix with a pastry dough blender until combined. Add essential oils and mix well.

TO USE: Use fun tools and toys to play in the sand and mold creations.

TO STORE: Store indefinitely in a covered container.

AROMATHERAPY PLAYDOUGH

Making your own playdough at home is fun and economical! The essential oils in this recipe make for an experience bursting with fragrance.

YIELD: Approximately 1 cup

1 cup flour, plus more as needed

1 cup distilled water

¼ cup salt

2 teaspoons cream of tartar

1 tablespoon vegetable oil

1-3 drops food coloring

20 drops essential oils of choice (lavender, peppermint, and orange are great choices)

TO MAKE: Combine all ingredients, except essential oils, in a pot on the stove. Cook over medium-low heat, stirring constantly, until mixture forms a ball. Remove from pot and place on a cutting board until cool, then add in your chosen essential oils. Knead the dough until smooth. If it's too sticky, add a little extra flour.

TO USE: Use hands or molds to make shapes and play with this fun dough!

TO STORE: Store for up to 1 month in an airtight container in a cool, dark place.

SUPER SOFT PLAYDOUGH

There are so many variations of playdough you could make, but this is one of the easiest and quickest. Divide your dough into four equal parts and add in different essential oils to your liking. I like using lavender, orange, peppermint, and lemon; they all have great, uplifting, happy qualities that your kids will love!

YIELD: 1½ cups

3 cups cornstarch, plus more as needed

1½ cups all-natural hair conditioner (such as Dr. Bronner's or Burt's Bees)

30 drops essential oils of choice (lavender, orange, peppermint, and lemon are great choices)

TO MAKE: Combine cornstarch and conditioner in a large bowl. Mix together until it forms a nice ball. Depending on your conditioner, you may need to add a little more cornstarch if it seems too wet. Turn it out onto a cutting board and knead well. Add in your chosen essential oils.

TO USE: Use hands or molds to make shapes and play with this fun dough!

TO STORE: Store for up to 1 month in an airtight container in a cool, dark place.

BE HAPPY PLAYDOUGH

Whip up a batch of Be Happy Playdough with the "happy" scent of citrus essential oils. This no-cook playdough is easy to make and will last up to a month of fun in an airtight container or zip-top bags.

YIELD: 2 cups

2 cups flour, plus more as needed

½ cup salt

1 tablespoon cream of tartar

2 tablespoons coconut oil, melted

1½ cups boiling water, plus more as needed

¼ cup glitter

10 drops lemon essential oil

10 drops lime essential oil

10 drops orange essential oil

TO MAKE: Combine flour, salt, cream of tartar, and coconut oil in a large bowl. Mix well with a fork. Carefully pour in boiling water. Stir until mixture forms a ball. If the consistency seems off, add either more boiling water or more flour. Knead on a cutting board and add in glitter. Knead again and add in essential oils.

TO USE: Use hands or molds to make shapes and play with this fun dough!

TO STORE: Store for up to 1 month in an airtight container in a cool, dark place.

GLITTER SLIME

Kids love slime! Why not make your own at home and add essential oil to the mixture? This easy recipe with energizing, uplifting peppermint essential oil will quickly become a favorite in your house!

YIELD: Approximately 6 ounces

1 teaspoon borax

1 cup warm distilled water

1 (4-ounce) bottle Elmer's Classic Glitter Glue (any color)

15 drops peppermint essential oil

TO MAKE: Combine borax and water in a small bowl and stir well to dissolve. Next, add the glue to a large bowl. Add a small amount of the borax mixture to the glue bottle and shake to get the last little bits of glue out. Add the borax mixture to the glue and mix well with a spoon. Once the ingredients are mostly incorporated, use your hands to mix the rest of the way. Stop mixing once it has reached a pliable "slime" consistency. Add in peppermint essential oil and mix well.

TO USE: Use hands to play with slime.

TO STORE: Store for up to 1 month in a covered jar or container.

DIY FLUBBER

Make this borax-free, bouncy, and stretchy DIY Flubber infused with peppermint and lavender essential oils for a quick and fun sensory experience!

YIELD: Approximately 12 ounces

2 (4-ounce) bottles Elmer's School Glue

1 cup liquid starch

15 drops lavender essential oil

15 drops peppermint essential oil

TO MAKE: Combine glue and liquid starch in a large bowl. Mix well. Add in lavender and peppermint essential oils. Knead with hands to get the consistency of a rubbery material that will stretch and bounce.

TO USE: Use hands to play with, stretch, and bend DIY Flubber.

TO STORE: Store in covered container for up to 1 month.

LAVENDER RICE FOR SENSORY PLAY

Lavender rice is a wonderful sensory play activity that your child can use to calm down and relax at the end of the day, or simply when things are just a little too crazy. Lavender calms and relaxes, which is why it's perfect in this recipe!

YIELD:1 pound lavender rice

2 tablespoons distilled water

2-3 drops purple gel food coloring (use more if you desire a darker color)

1 pound white rice

10 drops lavender essential oil

TO MAKE: Combine water and food coloring in a small bowl. Add rice to a separate large bowl. Add food-coloring mixture to rice and mix well. Once the color is evenly distributed, add in lavender essential oil and mix well. Pour the rice onto a large surface covered with paper towels and allow to dry.

TO USE: Once dry, add rice to a large pan and give to your kids to play with. You can add in small scoops or toys, or they can just use their hands to enjoy!

TO STORE: Store indefinitely in a large covered container or zip-top bag. Refresh lavender scent as needed.

CALMING WATER BEADS

To help your child calm down at the end of the day, try these water beads. These little clear beads that fill with water and provide hydration to plants are a great calming tool when infused with lavender essential oil. You can use these beads again and again, anytime you need to help your child relax.

YIELD: 1 pack of beads

1 (2-ounce) package floral hydration aqua beads (can be found at any craft store)

Distilled water, as needed

5-6 drops lavender essential oil

TO MAKE: Place water beads in the bottom of a medium container. Fill container with water. Add lavender essential oil. Allow the beads to sit for several hours to absorb the water.

TO USE: Once the beads are full of the water, you can either leave in the water or drain it off. Allow your kids to use their hands to play with the beads to relax and unwind.

TO STORE: Place the beads in a covered container and cover them with distilled water. Use within 1 week.

FOCUS SPRAY

Whenever you need your child to be focused, try this all-natural solution with peppermint and grapefruit essential oils. Both oils are known for their ability to clear the mind and uplift the senses. It's the perfect combination to put you and/or your child in a clear state of mind!

YIELD: ¼ cup

¼ cup distilled water

10 drops peppermint essential oil

10 drops grapefruit essential oil

TO MAKE: Combine all ingredients in a small spray bottle. Shake well.

TO USE: Spray into center of room to create a clear and focused mind!

TO STORE: Store indefinitely in spray bottle.

FUSSY BABY CALMER

Lavender is known to calm and relax in no time! Try this little trick to get your baby to relax and fall asleep the all-natural way.

YIELD: 1 application of Fussy Baby Calmer

1 drop lavender essential oil

TO MAKE: Apply 1 drop of lavender essential oil to an item in the baby's crib area.

TO USE: Place scented item near the baby to provide the calming aromatherapy benefits of lavender.

CALMING BEDTIME SPRAY

To create an environment that is conducive to sleep, try this all-natural bedtime spray. Lavender and chamomile essential oils both have calming properties, making them perfect for putting your baby in a sleepy state of mind.

YIELD: ¼ cup

¼ cup distilled water

10 drops lavender essential oil

10 drops chamomile essential oil

TO MAKE: Combine all ingredients in a small spray bottle. Shake well.

TO USE: Spray in center of room, or on sheets, drapes, or carpet, to provide a lasting, relaxing scent.

TO STORE: Store indefinitely in spray bottle.

GUM-SOOTHING OIL

This simple recipe will help your baby relax and remain calm while providing pain relief for sore gums. Clove essential oil has pain-relieving properties, making it a wonderful, all-natural option for soothing soreness safely!

YIELD: 2 tablespoons

2 tablespoons olive oil

1 drop clove essential oil

TO MAKE: Combine olive oil and clove essential oil in a small dish or glass bottle.

TO USE: Using fingertip or a cotton swap, apply 1 drop of mixture to baby's gums.

TO STORE: Store indefinitely in covered dish or bottle in a cool, dark place.

DIAPER WIPES

Making your own diaper wipes is eco-friendly and easy on your budget. Try this nontoxic diaper wipe recipe that uses lavender essential oil to soothe and tea tree essential oil to purify on contact!

YIELD: 1 roll of wipes

1 roll high-quality paper towels

2 cups distilled water

1 tablespoon liquid Castile soap

1 tablespoon fractionated coconut oil

10 drops lavender essential oil

3 drops tea tree essential oil

TO MAKE: Lay the paper towel roll horizontally on the table in front of you, then use a serrated knife to cut the roll in half. Use one half of roll now and keep one half of roll for next use. Combine water, soap, coconut oil, and essential oils in a bowl. Mix well. Remove the cardboard tube from the paper towel roll and discard, then place paper towel roll half in a plastic container (like an empty baby wipes container). Pour the water mixture over the paper towels and allow to sit for 10 minutes.

TO USE: Pull wipes from the center of the roll and use for diaper changes in place of commercial wipes.

TO STORE: Store for up to 2 weeks in covered container.

DIAPER CREAM

This easy Diaper Cream is wonderful to use at every diaper change to keep skin clear. The lavender and tea tree essential oils ensure that your baby's skin is soothed and protected naturally!

YIELD: 1 cup

1 cup coconut oil

½ ounce beeswax

10 drops lavender essential oil

10 drops tea tree essential oil

TO MAKE: Melt together coconut oil and beeswax in a small pot over medium heat. Stir until smooth. Remove from heat and let cool for 5–10 minutes. Add in lavender and tea tree essential oils and mix well. Pour into a small jar with a lid and allow to harden before use, approximately 1 hour.

TO USE: Apply liberally to baby's bottom during diaper changes.

TO STORE: Store indefinitely in jar in a cool, dark location.

LAVENDER AND CHAMOMILE DIAPER CREAM

Teething, diet changes, and medications can all cause babies' skin to be uncomfortable. Treat it naturally with this lavender diaper cream. Lavender and chamomile essential oils soothe the skin while providing a purifying defense. Your baby will be happy and comfortable in no time!

YIELD: 1 cup

1 cup coconut oil

½ ounce beeswax

1 teaspoon zinc oxide powder

10 drops lavender essential oil

10 drops chamomile essential oil

TO MAKE: Melt together coconut oil and beeswax in a small pot over medium heat. Stir until smooth. Add in zinc oxide powder and mix well. Remove from heat and let cool for 5–10 minutes. Stir in lavender and chamomile essential oils. Pour into a small jar with a lid and allow to harden before use, approximately 1 hour.

TO USE: Apply liberally to baby's bottom during diaper changes.

TO STORE: Store indefinitely in jar in a cool, dark location.

CLOTH DIAPER–SAFE DIAPER CREAM

This Cloth Diaper-Safe Diaper Cream will provide a protective barrier against wetness without ruining your cloth diapers like traditional diaper creams that repel wetness and cause leaks in your diapers. Nourishing and soothing, this diaper cream with lavender and tea tree essential oils will quickly become your favorite!

YIELD: 1 cup

½ cup coconut oil

¼ cup shea butter

¼ cup cocoa butter

½ ounce beeswax

10 drops lavender essential oil

10 drops tea tree essential oil

TO MAKE: Make a double boiler by simmering a small amount of water in a pot on the stove. Place a metal bowl slightly smaller than the pot over the water, then add coconut oil, shea butter, cocoa butter, and beeswax to the bowl. Stir until smooth. Remove from heat and allow to cool for 5–10 minutes. Add in lavender and tea tree essential oils and mix well. Pour into a small jar with a lid and allow to harden before use, approximately 1 hour.

TO USE: Apply liberally to baby's bottom during diaper changes.

TO STORE: Store indefinitely in jar in a cool, dark location.

FISH TANK ODOR DESTROYER

While you may not be able to put something in your fish tank to remove odors without messing up the environment, you can use essential oils outside the tank to freshen things up! Lemon and lime essential oils are great at removing odors the natural way.

YIELD: 1 air freshener

10 drops lemon essential oil

10 drops lime essential oil

⅛ cup distilled water

1 empty commercial plug-in air freshener container

TO MAKE: Take the wick out of your old plug-in. Fill the container about ½ full with lemon and lime essential oils. Fill the remainder of the plug-in with distilled water. Replace the wick.

TO USE: Plug into wall outlet near fish tank and use as normal.

PET CAGE FRESHENER

Keep your room smelling clean by using this Pet Cage Freshener each time you clean your pet's cage. Lemon essential oil will remove odors to keep things smelling fresh!

YIELD: 3 cups, or 1 application of Pet Cage Freshener

2 cups water

1 cup vinegar

½ cup baking soda

10 drops lemon essential oil

TO MAKE: Combine all ingredients in a large bowl or bucket. Mix well.

TO USE: Scrub your pet's entire cage with the solution to get it clean and odor-free. Rinse well after use.

CARPET PET STAIN REMOVER

Pet stains are a thing of the past with this nontoxic pet stain remover! Lemon and orange essential oils purify and cut through stains easily on carpet.

YIELD: 2 cups, or 1 application of Carpet Pet Stain Remover

1 cup water

1 cup vinegar

1 cup baking soda

10 drops lemon essential oil

10 drops orange essential oil

TO MAKE: Combine water and vinegar in a spray bottle. Shake well. Combine baking soda and essential oils in a bowl. Mix well.

TO USE: Sprinkle baking-soda mixture over stain, then pour the water mixture over the baking soda. It will foam up and work on the stain. Let it sit for 5–10 minutes, then blot with a clean paper towel.

URINE REMOVER

Get rid of urine stains with this foaming carpet cleaning solution. Vinegar and baking soda work to destroy odors on contact, and lemon essential oil takes this basic cleaner a step further by purifiying the surface and working to break down any leftover odors and stains.

YIELD: 2 cups, or 1 application of Urine Remover

1 cup distilled water

1 cup vinegar

1 cup baking soda

20 drops lemon essential oil

TO MAKE: Combine water and vinegar in a spray bottle. Shake well. Combine baking soda and lemon essential oil in a bowl. Mix well.

TO USE: Blot up as much of the urine as possible with dry paper towels. After blotting up the excess urine, sprinkle baking-soda mixture over stain. Then, pour the water mixture over the baking soda. It will foam up and work on the stain. Let it sit for 5–10 minutes, then blot with a clean paper towel. Once dry, vacuum area.

U.S./METRIC CONVERSION CHART

VOLUME CONVERSIONS

U.S. Volume Measure	Metric Equivalent
⅛ teaspoon	0.5 milliliter
¼ teaspoon	1 milliliter
½ teaspoon	2 milliliters
1 teaspoon	5 milliliters
½ tablespoon	7 milliliters
1 tablespoon (3 teaspoons)	15 milliliters
2 tablespoons (1 fluid ounce)	30 milliliters
¼ cup (4 tablespoons)	60 milliliters
⅓ cup	90 milliliters
½ cup (4 fluid ounces)	125 milliliters
⅔ cup	160 milliliters
¾ cup (6 fluid ounces)	180 milliliters
1 cup (16 tablespoons)	250 milliliters
1 pint (2 cups)	500 milliliters
1 quart (4 cups)	1 liter (about)

WEIGHT CONVERSIONS

U.S. Weight Measure	Metric Equivalent
½ ounce	15 grams
1 ounce	30 grams
2 ounces	60 grams
3 ounces	85 grams
¼ pound (4 ounces)	115 grams
½ pound (8 ounces)	225 grams
¾ pound (12 ounces)	340 grams
1 pound (16 ounces)	454 grams

OVEN TEMPERATURE CONVERSIONS

Degrees Fahrenheit	Degrees Celsius
200 degrees F	95 degrees C
250 degrees F	120 degrees C
275 degrees F	135 degrees C
300 degrees F	150 degrees C
325 degrees F	160 degrees C
350 degrees F	180 degrees C
375 degrees F	190 degrees C
400 degrees F	205 degrees C
425 degrees F	220 degrees C
450 degrees F	230 degrees C

LENGTH CONVERSIONS

U.S. Length Measure	Metric Equivalent
¼ inch	0.6 centimeter
½ inch	1.2 centimeters
¾ inch	1.9 centimeters
1 inch	2.5 centimeters
1½ inches	3.8 centimeters
1 foot	0.3 meter
1 yard	0.9 meter

INDEX

ABOUT THE AUTHOR

KASEY SCHWARTZ was born and raised in West Virginia before moving to Illinois in 1999 where she met her husband-to-be and laid down roots. After Kasey became a wife and mom of three, she started the blog *All Things Mamma* (*http:// allthingsmamma.com*) to talk about her family experiences and favorite products in hopes of helping other moms, and even learn a little more herself. Even in the early days of *All Things Mamma*, Kasey focused on green and clean solutions in her home and family. As she gained more experience as a mom of three, she also gained experience in leading a natural lifestyle, and she started using essential oils more in her everyday life. Kasey was first introduced to essential oils fifteen years ago while studying to become a massage therapist, and she has since become an expert on using them in her home, from treating her family naturally for health ailments to cooking, cleaning, and household remedies. Kasey now stays home with her family and blogs full-time at *All Things Mamma*, where she shares tips and tricks for making life easier and green recipes, reviews, and crafts. Her experience has landed her interviews for Sinclair Broadcasting's *Family 411* weekly syndication and several local news stations. Kasey has also been featured on BetterHomesandGardens .com, Wayfair.com, ExtraordinaryMommy.com, ScaryMommy.com, Momdot.com, TopMomBlogger.com, *Mom Talk Radio*, SurvivingtheStores.com, and a variety of other websites.